JUSTICE FOR THE UNBORN

Justice for the Unborn

Why We Have "Legal" Abortion, and How We Can Stop It

Randall J. Hekman

SERVANT BOOKS
Ann Arbor, Michigan

Cover and book design by John B. Leidy
Cover photo by H. Armstrong Roberts

Available from Servant Books, Box 8617, Ann Arbor, Michigan 48107

ISBN 0-89283-194-4
Printed in the United States of America

1 2 3 4 5 6 7 8 9 10 89 88 87 86 85 84

Library of Congress Cataloging in Publication Data

Hekman, Randall J.
Justice for the Unborn.

Includes index.
1. Abortion—United States. 2. Abortion—United States—Moral and ethical aspects. 3. Abortion—Law and legislation—United States. I. Title.
HQ767.5.U5H43 1984 363.4'6 84-5424
ISBN 0-89283-194-4

To my beloved wife, Marcia, whose faith and courage as my best friend and the mother of our eight children makes me admire her more and more as the years fly by.

Acknowledgments

My thanks to those who encouraged me in writing this book: my wife, my children and my parents as well as Dr. Bill Bright.

I am also appreciative for the use of Calvin College's library in performing some of the research for this book.

James Manney of Servant Publications provided many invaluable comments regarding my original manuscript for which I am grateful.

Above all, I thank God for allowing me to be used by him in writing this book. Without doubt, children are a priority to God and dear to his loving heart.

—Randall J. Hekman

Contents

ONE

My World Turned Upside Down

"JUDGE, THE CASEWORKER for Jane Doe says that Jane is pregnant and wants an abortion."

My hearing coordinator, Deborah Kammer, could see me emotionally recoil to what she had just said.

"That's an issue between her and her mother," I replied, somewhat curtly. "The court in general and me in particular want nothing to do with abortions."

I knew my answer was correct at least on the surface of things. A law in Michigan where I serve as a Juvenile Court Judge makes it clear that parents alone have the total discretion over whether or not to approve elective surgery for their children.[1] This requested abortion was not to save the life of the 13-year-old, but for "cosmetic" reasons.

Jane Doe (not her real name) became a temporary neglect ward of our court at a hearing on August 18, 1982. On that date, her mother acknowledged in open court that she had not been providing an emotionally stable home for her daughter and sought help from the court to handle Jane's unmanageable behavior. Jane had run away from home many times and was not obeying her mother's rules. For her 13 years, Jane was very streetwise and physically mature. Jane's father was a "nowhere man."

At the August hearing, we had no idea that Jane was pregnant. Her caseworker, looking merely to the strained mother-daughter relationship, recommended one last attempt at a placement home with the mother under court supervision and counseling. If it failed, removal and placement of Jane elsewhere would have to be done.

Since the prognosis was questionable, I decided to adjourn the case for two months until October 19, 1982 and, in the meantime, allow Jane to return home under supervision. If things did not work out, I could then remove Jane from her mother's home and place her in a foster or group home.

In September, much to my growing consternation, Jane's caseworker began informing the court by phone that Jane was pregnant and wanted the court to get her an abortion. While I was not overly surprised hearing that a court ward was pregnant (it, unfortunately, happens with all too great regularity), never before in the history of our court had a ward sought court assistance in procuring an abortion. All other abortions of pregnant teens appearing before our court have occurred following parental authorization totally independent of the court. We typically hear about the abortions *after* they have been done.

But Jane's father was unavailable and her mother refused to sign the abortion approval. Since Jane was a ward of our court, no abortion clinic would perform the abortion without authorization from a parent or the court.

My initial response to Jane's request was to fend off the caseworker's inquiry and hope that the issue would somehow resolve itself without a need for court involvement. Yet, deep inside, I felt that this case would not merely go away but would dog my heels relentlessly.

I have been a juvenile court judge since January, 1975. My duties primarily involve families with problems. Young people who have broken the law appear before me as do parents who have neglected or abused their children. Juvenile court judges are given wide discretion to administer the sometimes elusive quality we call justice with the hopes of helping those in need and protecting society as well.[2]

The caseworker was caught in a difficult situation. On the one hand, she had responsibility to make plans for a five-months-pregnant, 13-year-old who insisted she wanted an abortion. On the other hand, the caseworker was running headlong into a court which said it had no authority in this type of a case, a mother who would not give her approval, and abortion clinics who would not act without the signature of a judge or parent. Also, the clock was ticking, making any abortion increasingly more difficult to obtain.

The court had appointed Attorney E. Lou Hoos to represent the interests of Jane for her August court hearing. In September, the caseworker turned to Lou for help. Lou realized the only possible way out of the dilemma was to petition the court to authorize the abortion.

On October 13, while I was on recess between court hearings, Lou approached me in a hallway at Juvenile Court and told me the news I definitely did not want to hear.

"Have we got a rough case for you coming next week," Lou said with a slight chuckle. "I represent Jane Doe who wants an abortion so bad she can taste it," he continued. "We're going to have to file a petition with the court asking for the abortion."

I took a deep breath. My mouth went dry. I invited Lou into my office and quickly told him that the law was very unclear whether a juvenile court judge even had the authority to order an abortion over the objections of a girl's parents.

Lou did not challenge my assessment of the law; he indicated that he himself was unsure about the law in this uncharted area. But he felt he had no choice but to bring the petition in light of his client's insistence.

"Also, Lou," I continued, "I've got a real problem with abortion." Lou, an attorney I respect and have worked with for many years, seemed to let my last statement bounce off without sinking in. Pressed for time, he soon left.

My heart was numb; I found myself saying a quick prayer for strength. I put on my black judicial robe and returned to the courtroom adjoining my chambers for the next in my series of court hearings that afternoon. But my mind kept wandering from the testimony of witnesses and statements of attorneys.

I felt waves of panic attempt to overwhelm me on the inside while I forced myself to make decisions for the people in front of me. Judges do not have the luxury of letting bad days get to them; there is too much at stake. I think I did reasonably well that afternoon despite my tumultuous emotions. But, whenever a lull in the testimony allowed my attention to wane, I found my heart repeatedly asking God, "What am I going to do?"

The next few days, in every spare moment, I did little other than ponder my upcoming case. I sought the counsel of friends, fellow judges, lawyers, and others, both locally and elsewhere. I knew it would be wrong to order an abortion since this was the deliberate killing of a human, unborn child. As a Christian, I cannot purposefully do that which violates God's standards. But, as a judge, I did not know how I should *legally* respond to the forthcoming petition for the abortion. And, as a human being, I do not particularly enjoy hassles.

I was elected Probate Court Judge in 1974 at the ripe old age of twenty-seven. For the two years prior to that, I served as an Assistant Prosecutor for Kent County (Grand Rapids) Michigan. In this position, I represented the people of Michigan in many courts, including Kent County Juvenile Court which is a division of Probate Court.

As an Assistant Prosecutor, I appreciated many outstanding aspects of the Juvenile Court, but I was disappointed with what I considered to be an inadequate response to serious juvenile crime. As a result, I prayerfully considered a rather significant step: challenging a highly respected incumbent judge at the next election on the sole issue of dealing more effectively with serious juvenile crime. With much fear and trepidation, yet with a settled heart that what I was doing was ultimately the right thing to do, I threw my hat in the ring.

My basic approach in campaigning was to say, "If you agree with me that Juvenile Court needs changing, vote for me; if you disagree, please vote for my very able opponent who has more experience than I."

News media coverage of the very colorful campaign gave me much free advertising. I was amazed that our campaign expenses of close to $8,000 were paid for by hundreds of mostly small donations. All that I had to contribute at the end to balance the books was $48 (which was fortunate since I didn't have much more than that to give at the time).

Everyone including myself was surprised when I was elected with 54 percent of the vote in November 1974. I was also gratified that the governor thereafter appointed the man I defeated to be a probate judge in a neighboring county. He enjoys his new job. While our relationship was strained during the campaign, we now enjoy an open, warm relationship.

The real hard part began after the election. It's one thing to stand on the outside and say how Juvenile Court should be different; it's quite another to make the changes. My experience was that no real changes did take place despite all my valiant efforts until I committed the problems to God. Then I saw rapid changes. Specific programs that have been instituted at least in part through my influence during the past eight years are:

1. Sending letters to victims of crime inquiring as to the amount of their loss so that restitution can be ordered where feasible.

2. Introducing a community service work program for certain offenders to pay back the community for their violations.

3. Establishing criteria which assure that those who have committed serious crimes, offenders who formerly might have been dismissed at the intake level, must now come before the judges.

4. Establishing a "Youth Camp" treatment facility for

repeat juvenile offenders. This involved the miraculous raising of $150,000 in about ten days and building a high-quality structure in a few short weeks.

5. Establishing a comprehensive program to respond more appropriately to child sexual abuse cases.

I do not want to convey that I have made no mistakes or that I have never gone down blind alleys. I certainly have. More times than I care to remember I have had to seek the forgiveness of God and others for impatient and unloving attitudes. I have also found it easy to fall into the trap of misplaced priorities: putting my work ahead of my wife and children. And then there was the time in 1978 when I ran unsuccessfully for a higher judicial post. Just as God can say yes, he can also say an emphatic no.

Overall, however, I have thoroughly enjoyed my job—especially the challenges of the various projects described above.

In September and early October of 1982, things were going particularly well—almost too well. My job was beginning to feel easy. I remember remarking to my case aide, Deb Kammer and my secretary-court recorder, Marilyn King, "Things are getting so easy that I'm actually getting bored. It's about time for a new challenge."

Little did I know that God had one of the hardest challenges of my life waiting for me just around the corner.

As my office began to receive the insistent calls regarding Jane Doe and her desired abortion, I sensed God telling me, "Get ready, Randy, a real test is coming your way."

Come my way it did. Over the past eight years, I had occasionally wondered what I would do if ever I was asked to order an abortion. As a Christian who belives that God himself creates people in the womb,[3] I knew that I could never order the killing of an unborn child simply because someone wanted it done. But how would I respond *legally* to such a request? Would I resign or disqualify myself? Such questions troubled me. I would simply hope it would never happen and dismiss the issue from my mind.

But God *did* let it happen. His overruling providence can clearly be seen. Of the four judges currently in our court, I was the one to pick the "short straw."

When Attorney Hoos told me the abortion petition was coming, my first reaction was to throw this "hot potato" to another judge and disqualify myself from the case. After all, I reasoned, I am well known in my community as a devout Christian and was even identified in a September 1982 article in our local newspaper as a participant in a Michigan Right-to-Life Conference. I thought I should probably step aside for the sake of the court (not to mention my own skin).

But the more I considered disqualification the more I realized that such would be wrong. After all, I asked myself, why should a judge who is required by law to protect young children from child abuse be considered a bad judge simply because he won't order the brutal slaying of an unborn child? Do we want schizophrenic juvenile judges who can order the killing of unborn children while enthusiastically protecting other children who make it to birth? I hope not.

A judge should disqualify himself when he cannot in good conscience enter an order required by the law. My initial reading of the law about abortion led me to conclude that a judge in my position must altogether ignore the rights of the unborn child in making the abortion decision. Since taking this position would be intellectually and morally repugnant to me, it seemed at first that I should step aside. But is this really *the* law?

I discussed an analogous situation with friend and colleague Judge John P. Steketee. In Hitler's Germany it was once totally *legal* to torture, maim, and kill Jews. But after the war, those who did such atrocities were tried by a higher law and punished. As we shall later see, abortion irrefutably involves the unlawful and unjust taking of innocent human lives.

I felt I *was* able to obey and enforce the ultimate law implied by the Nuremberg trials, those immutable principles that eternally exist irrespective of man's transitory attempts to overrule and ignore them.

Finally, I realized that disqualification would not absolve me from a moral dilemma. If I voluntarily hand a case over to another judge who I know could order what I believe to be a grossly unjust act, I would still be a conscious and willing part of the ultimate injustice. If I say, in effect, "I can't shoot that baby, but I'll give the loaded gun to someone who will," I am implicated in the ultimate crime.

For these reasons, I decided I could not and should not voluntarily disqualify myself.

But how would I rule? What standard of law should I apply? And if I find I cannot follow the law issued by the Supreme Court, ought I to resign?

TWO

My Decision

DURING THE WEEKEND before the fateful court hearing, I prayed that Jane or her attorney would change their minds. Thus far it had been only talk. Courts need not act unless a petition or request is formally filed in writing or otherwise is made in open court.

On Sunday, I taught our adult Sunday School class on how God uses trials in our lives to help us grow more Christlike. I told the class about my upcoming case as an illustration and requested prayer for wisdom and courage.

Despite my eleventh-hour hopes that the case would disappear, on Monday, October 18, 1982, Attorney Hoos filed his "Petition for Court Authorization for Abortion." As I held the petition in my hand and read, I sighed and shook my head slowly. There was now no turning back.

By coincidence, Jane Doe's adjourned disposition hearing had been scheduled for the following day, October 19, for thirty minutes. Obviously, with the new abortion request attached to the original issue of placement for Jane, the hearing would likely take longer than previously anticipated. However, I wanted to make my decision as quickly as possible to keep the emotion-packed case from being tried in the media should they become aware of the situation. The decision would be hard enough without thousands of arm chair quarterbacks calling the plays from the sidelines.

The night before the hearing, my wife Marcia and I prayed diligently for God's wisdom. I told her the same thing I had told my staff: that my decision in this case could easily cost me my job since a state agency exists with the power to remove "errant" judges from the bench. It might even cost me my freedom should I be placed in the position of defying a higher court's order.

Marcia, my courageous wife, expressed what I felt: "You've got to do what is right regardless of the consequences. God will take care of you if you do." Those of our children old enough to understand started to pray vigorously for me. But they had a difficult time comprehending how I as a judge could get into trouble for "not killing a baby in a mommy's tummy." Children can be so logical sometimes.

Another fascinating development was that Jane Doe's mother called her favorite TV station informing them that an "abortion case" involving her daughter was coming before me the next day. As a result, a reporter from the station appeared at court.

Because our proceedings are usually confidential, Juvenile Court is typically off the beaten track for news people. In fact, it had been two years since there had been news coverage of any case in my court. Had the mother not called her station, I doubt that any news coverage of the case would have occurred. I would have given my decision to a handful of people in my courtroom, and that would probably have been the end of it. However, again, God had other plans.

But what was I going to do? Having decided not to disqualify myself, my next legal hurdle was to determine what standard of law a judge ought to use in such a case. Many legal issues relating to abortion are well established, but the criteria a Michigan juvenile court judge should use in ruling on a minor's abortion request is far from clear.

I am a firm believer in seeking "creative alternatives" when placed in a situation where I might have to disobey the wishes of those in authority over me. When we maintain a submissive attitude, we can often discover an innovative way to remain subservient and yet not violate our ethical and moral standards.

The Bible gives an excellent example of this principle in the first chapter of the book of Daniel. Daniel was told to eat of the king's meat and drink his wine. To obey this command would violate Daniel's religious scruples. Rather than foolishly defying the king with the Babylonian equivalent of "No way, Jose," Daniel very wisely suggested a creative alternative—a ten-day experiment in which he and his friends would eat only vegetables and drink only water.

Since the man in authority over Daniel didn't really care what Daniel and his friends ate as long as they physically flourished, Daniel was able, with God's grace, to satisfy both God and the king.

It is easy for us in taking a stand for principles to do so in a way that unnecessarily antagonizes those in authority. We feel smug and self-righteous in so "suffering for Christ," but, in reality, we are being very foolish and are suffering for our own sakes.

I must quickly point out that creative alternatives are not always available. Later in Daniel's life, he deliberately disobeyed the law and was thrown to the lions (see Daniel 6). Still, God protected him.

As I poured over the law books that Monday night, I earnestly sought and prayed for a creative alternative—some loophole or plausible legal argument whereby I could legally give due regard for the rights of the unborn child in making my decision. However, I could find none.

However, one tempting possibility did emerge as I studied the law. Various U.S. Supreme Court decisions on abortion and related issues seemed to require that a judge first determine if the pregnant girl was mature enough to make the abortion decision for herself. If she was not mature, the court was to give the girl the opportunity to show that the abortion would nonetheless be in her best interests. If she was sufficiently mature, the court was to allow her to make the abortion decision on her own.

Now, if the facts of my case proved that Jane was too immature to make the decision for herself and that it would *not* serve her best interests to have the abortion, I could simply apply the law as given and not be required to order the abortion. I was quite sure that the testimony in court was in fact going to be along these lines: that Jane was immature and that the abortion would *not* be in her best interests irrespective of the unborn child's rights.

Was this perhaps the "creative alternative" which would allow me to obey both God and the law? It was certainly tempting to consider applying the law as I construed it and to deny the abortion on the facts presented. But my conscience would not permit me this enticing alternative.

For a judge to hide his true feelings about a crucial matter from the litigants concerned is fundamentally dishonest. Also, for me to state publicly that my ruling was based only on Jane Doe's best interests would make me vulnerable to the accusation that I actually had let my widely-known pro-life "biases" enter into the judicial equation, even if this were not technically true.

Further, I doubted that I would ever again be able to speak out publicly against abortion for fear that my "biases" would be exposed, opening me up to renewed criticism for the court decision.

I could also envision a reporter asking an unanswerable question: "Judge Hekman, you attended the Michigan Right-to-Life Conference last month. Could you as a judge *ever* order an abortion?"

If I answered "No," I would be subject to justified criticism for ruling on Jane's abortion request. If I answered "Yes," I would be lying. If I answered with a "No comment," I may as well pack my bags.

After wrestling with the issues until about 4:00 A.M. the morning of the hearing, I finally went to bed for two fitful hours.

At 6:00, I got up and hurriedly wrote my feelings and thoughts regarding the law. I decided it was going to be all or nothing. I was going to be honest and bold with the legal issues. I would explain how the U.S. Supreme Court's abortion decision in 1973 was illogical and contrary to the actual spirit and language of the Constitution. I would allude to the concepts of "higher Law" relied upon at Nuremburg.

That Tuesday morning I heard testimony on the case. Literally ***all*** the evidence presented was to the effect that an abortion would ***not*** serve the girl's best interests because of the guilt she would thereafter suffer. Jane offered no comments and no witnesses of her own.

I gave my opinion on the record. Appendix A is an edited transcript of the opinion.

As I left the courtroom, I felt a great sense of relief. Ever since the Supreme Court made its landmark pro-abortion decision in *Roe* v. *Wade* [1] in 1973, I have been privately and publicly critical of its ruling and the reasoning for it. Yet I have been as helpless as anyone to stop the killing of the unborn in our country. But now I was able to stand against the bloodshed in my own small way and say, "No, this baby will not join the other millions in death; this baby will live if I have anything to do with it." I also felt a bit like David against Goliath. I, a lowly trial judge, was standing against the authority of the U.S. Supreme Court, knowing that ultimate justice and ***the*** law were on my side.

The TV reporter was waiting for me. Since I had ruled on the case that Tuesday morning, I was legally and ethically free to make public comments explaining the decision.[2] Neither Jane's attorney nor the prosecutor wanted any outsiders in the courtroom, so the TV news reporter had to wait outside. After making my decision, I gave him a statement. I said that the decision was based on the best interests of ***both*** the 13-year-old girl ***and*** the unborn child. Not being well versed on the law of abortion, the reporter did not initially see the significance of the decision as breaking new legal ground.

But the story went on the air that night—the only news

coverage of the case on that first day. It would have ended there but for an alert *Grand Rapids Press* reporter who heard about the case from a fellow worker who happened to see the TV news. The reporter called me the next morning. I gave her excerpts from my opinion over the telephone which she then released to the wire services, carrying it to other news agencies around the country.

For the next few days, I was responding virtually nonstop to TV, radio, and newspaper interviews. Sometimes this pace was exhilarating; sometimes it was unnerving.

Many nights, I lay awake thinking about the many issues. Gradually I realized I was worrying about many things completely outside my control. While I found it relatively easy to trust God to give me the words to say to reporters, I would then worry about how the reporters would prepare their stories, how their editors would put them together, and how the public would repond to the edited stories.

God made it clear to me to trust him to take care of those things outside my control. It is wrong for me to worry about that which is not my responsibility. God wants me to experience his peace (Phil 4:6-7).

One thing I particularly did not want was an appeal of my decision. However, goaded in large part by the extent and tenor of the media coverage and the vocal protests of pro-abortionists, Attorney Lou Hoos and his client decided to appeal.

The necessary papers, transcript and my opinion were prepared for the appeal in almost record time. The appeal was heard and decided by Judge Robert Benson of the Kent County Circuit Court on October 28, 1982.

I had hoped that Judge Benson would at most criticize some of the strong anti-abortion language in my opinion, but nonetheless uphold me on the grounds that the facts of the case would require even a pro-abortion judge to rule against the abortion.

I heard indirectly that the American Civil Liberties Union (ACLU) had also been talking to Lou Hoos. The ACLU wanted Lou to attempt to persuade Judge Benson to reopen the record so that testimony could be presented in favor of the abortion. Apparently the ACLU has access to "hired-gun experts" who will testify that abortions are always indicated for 13-year-old girls. In the initial hearing, Hoos had chosen to present no testimony.

Judge Benson did not do what I hoped he would. He ruled that Jane Doe could have a new hearing on her abortion request before a judge who would not have any preconceived notions as to the wrongfulness of abortion. He sent the case back to Juvenile Court with the instructions that it be heard by another judge who would have the authority to decide whether or not to reopen the record. Back in our court, the case was assigned to my friend and colleague, Judge Donald J. DeYoung. It is an understatement to say that Judge DeYoung did not welcome the case with open arms.

While the appeal was pending, I was going through an increasingly burdensome emotional nightmare. I came to the point where I seriously considered resigning my job to protest a law that seemed to require juvenile court judges to place unborn children on death row.

To resolve this issue, I fasted and prayed one day to obtain God's wisdom on whether to quit. I was left with the firm conviction that I was not only morally right but ultimately *legally* right to do what I did. No, I would not quit; I would fight this to the end! Having made the decision, I was left with a deep sense of peace.

While the appeal was pending, Jane began to see things in a new light. I had ordered her into a foster home on October 19 as her social worker recommended. While her caseworker looked for the right long-term foster home, I put Jane in a short-term facility called a shelter home.

Jane's experienced shelter home parents soon developed a

good rapport with her. She began to open up and talk about why she wanted an abortion.

Apparently, this decision was prompted by one of Jane's distant relatives from Detroit who called the shelter home and asked to speak to Jane. Jane said she was willing to talk. The relative told Jane that her baby has feet, hands, and already moves. The woman said, "It is not a fetus, a thing, a blob, but it is a child—just a matter of size." She also told Jane that "abortion hurts the baby."[12]

After this phone conversation, Jane began to ask the shelter parents various questions like, "What is abortion like?" and, "Can my baby feel pain?"

To help answer these questions, the shelter parents sought help from people who were more knowledgeable about abortion than they. Jane saw some films and had an ultrasound picture made of her child. The ultrasound showed her baby was a boy and that he was sucking his thumb. The procedure by which Jane obtained this information was not coercive, as a subsequent study by the Kent County Department of Social Services affirmed.[13]

As a result of this new information (and, undoubtedly, in answer to the prayers of many), on November 1 Jane told her school social worker she no longer wanted the abortion. She reaffirmed this change of heart to her guardian ad litem Douglas Lewis on November 2. When asked why she had wanted the abortion originally, Jane said, "People be talking about me and seeing me get bigger and I [am] too young to have a baby." She also said she was afraid her "heart would stop if I carried [my] child to full term." Where she received this information, I do not know.

Why did Jane change her mind? She told Mr. Lewis, "At first [I was] thinking only of me, now I feel [I] should also consider baby as well."[3]

Jane's decision to change her mind did not waver. Previously, she had been adamant about wanting the abortion.

Once she knew the facts, she was adamant about wanting to give birth.

On November 3, Jane and her attorneys appeared before Judge Donald DeYoung. It was abundantly clear that Jane had indeed changed her mind: she no longer wanted the abortion. In fact, Lou Hoos asked that the petition for abortion be withdrawn. Judge DeYoung also ruled that even if Jane had not changed her mind, the record in my case showed that it would still serve the best interests of Jane herself (apart from the rights of the unborn child) *not* to have the abortion.

I felt relieved and grateful for Jane's change of heart. I only wished that her caseworkers had given her enough information to make this enlightened decision *before* presenting me with the abortion request. Her worker's claim that Jane was not "ready" to listen to specifics on abortion earlier. That may well be true. Perhaps my comments and the hubbub surrounding the case started her thinking; I don't know. I do know that the additional time I gave her to consider the decision was definitely a factor in changing her mind.

Jane's change of heart also took some pressure off me. It diminished public sympathy for a pregnant 13-year-old who was supposedly being harrassed by an unfeeling judge with antiquated Victorian standards.

However, one issue didn't go away: may a trial judge, for the sake of the rights of an unborn child, spurn Supreme Court precedent which says that unborn children are legal non-entities? This issue soon mushroomed until I myself was on trial, as we shall see.

But before we get to that, let me share part of a letter Jane wrote to me on February 9, 1983:

> I am writing to tell you how happy I am that you made the decision you did about me not having an abortion. When I think about it now I feel sort of foolish, of that whole incident. . . . Right now, I am in a foster home that I sort of

like. We have our ups and downs but we get them together. I think if I would of gone ahead with the abortion, I would of felt very disappointed in myself. I just want to thank you for giving me the extra time to think about it. I am really looking towards having my baby. . . . I think you are a very intelligent and respective(sic) judge and my baby and I thank you very much!

THREE

The Judge on Trial

BEFORE ANY NEW DEVELOPMENT in the abortion case, God's Holy Spirit seemed to prepare me for it. Hence, when the event happened, I was not overly shocked and was usually somewhat prepared.

For example, when I first heard about the case, I had a deep sense of God telling me, "Get ready, Randy, here comes a challenge for you."

After the single television station reported on the case, I felt I wouldn't be surprised if a newspaper reporter picked up on the story and called me the next day. A reporter did.

After receiving the good news about Jane changing her mind, I half expected a negative newspaper editorial from our local *Grand Rapids Press* which had published pro-abortion editorials in the past.

I was right, but I was surprised at how extremely negative it was. The editorial appeared in the November 7, 1982 *Press* and was entitled "Judge Put Self Above the Law."

The editorial began with a right jab: "Kent County Probate Judge Randall Hekman is guilty of failure to step aside from a case on which he was biased and probably of blatant pandering to his political constituents." The author of the editorial went on to conclude that my motives in doing what I did were purely political. A copy of the editorial is printed in Appendix B. (I print it here not because I agree with it, but because it documents what painful consequences can follow difficult moral decisions.)

My initial reaction to the editorial was hurt and anger.

"If they only knew the agony I went through before making the decision," I told my wife and friends. "They imply I planned all this publicity." Perhaps the editorial writer was unaware that it was the *Press*'s own reporter who broadcasted the story over the wire services to the rest of the world.

I had simply made my decision before the parties in court; it was the media that broadcasted it beyond. Kalamazoo Probate Judge Donald Halstead had been severely criticized in his community for a similar decision in an abortion case a year before.[1] Thousands of people had signed petitions there to have him removed. I fully expected that sort of response for me. But I nonetheless made my decision because I was convinced it was the right thing to do.

As a Christian, I believe the Bible makes it clear that we are to say thank you to God for everything that happens to us, both good and bad.[2] The reason we can thank God in all things is found in Romans 8:28: "And we know that in all things God works for the good of those who love him, who have been called according to his purpose."

It was very hard for me to say thank you to God for this unkind editorial, but I did so nonetheless. And soon, with God's help, I saw the editorial not so much as a problem but as an opportunity to respond with a letter of my own to the newspaper.

I called the *Press* editors and told them I wished to provide a printed response for publication in their "Dissent!" column. I am grateful that they granted my request.

I worked on my response as time permitted. It was very hard to decide what to say. My wife Marcia stressed that I should not pay back evil with evil, but stick to the issues. I agreed.

While I was writing the response, another bombshell broke. On the morning of November 15, 1982, a *Press* reporter called to tell me that the local chapter of the National Organization for Women had just filed a complaint against me with the Michigan Judicial Tenure Commission. Perhaps I was paranoid, but I thought I detected some glee in the reporter's voice as she asked whether I wanted to make any response. After a few moments reflection, I gave her my reactions.

What this meant was that I as a judge was being placed on trial. Any citizen or group can file a complaint with the Michigan Judical Tenure Commission alleging judicial misconduct of any sitting judge on any issue.[3] The Tenure Commission investigates all complaints and then renders decisions. It can dismiss the charges, publicly or privately censure the judge, or suspend or permanently remove the judge from his duties. Any discipline, however, requires the concurrence of the Michigan Supreme Court.[4]

With all the power and discretion judges have been given, there is a continuing need for an organization such as the Judicial Tenure Commission.

"But the Tenure Commission disciplines judges who take bribes or are immoral or drunkards, not judges who refuse to kill babies," I found myself thinking. "This isn't fair."

As the reality of the complaint sunk in, I felt panicked.

"I ***am*** going to lose my job," I thought. "No, I won't let them fire me. I'll quit and do something else."

I finally found peace by saying to myself, "Look, when I made my decision I ***knew*** it could cost me my job. I made my decision nonetheless. Losing a job is a very small price to pay for saving a life. And God will take care of me."

Eventually I finished my editorial response for publication in the *Grand Rapids Press.* My fellow judges implored me to let the issue drop and ***not*** submit the article to the *Press.* They felt I could not win a war of words with the media. However, after much prayer and further discussion, I decided to give my response to the newspaper.

The *Press* indicated my draft response was twice as long as they were willing to publish, so I had to cut it virtually in half. A copy of my article, published in the *Press* on November 19, 1982, is reprinted in Appendix C.

Soon I could see the wisdom of God in leading me to submit my response. Readers of the *Press* reacted positively, as did many people to me directly. Even some members of my church said, "I thought you *had* made a mistake in not disqualifying yourself in that case until I read your article. You really had no choice."

My mail mushroomed during those days and letters continued to pour in for months. Since the beginning of the case, positive letters have outnumbered negative ones by more than 8 to 1.

My response to the *Press* editorial was reprinted in many other publications, including the *San Francisco Examiner,* the Christian Legal Society *Quarterly* and the *National Right to Life News.* It was cited in a supportive editorial in *Christianity Today.*[5]

God always gets the last word. What began as a very negative editorial for which I found it very difficult to thank God has opened many doors of opportunity. In fact, my decision to answer my critics has led to many new opportunities to speak and even certain awards have unexpectedly come as a result of this case. This has greatly encouraged me as well as others.

In early March, 1983, I submitted my legal response to the Michigan Judicial Tenure Commission. At some length, I developed a legal argument that would allow a judge who is presented with a petition for an abortion to give due consideration for the unborn child. The argument is essentially as follows:

1. There currently exists no binding legal precedent on the issue.

2. Even in *Roe* v *Wade* (the original 1973 case creating the right to abortion on demand), the Supreme Court acknowledged that the state *does* have a growing interest in

protecting the "potential life" of the unborn as the pregnancy develops.

3. *Roe* said the government may not proceed criminally against a *woman* nor her *physician* if she obtains an abortion prior to the seventh month of pregnancy. It did *not* say what a judge should do representing the state when *he* is making the decision.

4. Some recent Supreme Court decisions addressing the issue of whether the Constitution requires states to pay for Medicaid abortions have helpful language in them. For example, the 1977 case of *Maher* v *Roe* included the statement: "The State unquestionably has a strong and legitimate interest in encouraging normal childbirth, an interest honored over the centuries."[6] In *Harris* v *McRae* (1980), the Supreme Court held that

> the Hyde Amendment, by encouraging childbirth except in the most urgent circumstances, is rationallly related to the legitimate governmental objective of protecting potential life. . . .Abortion is inherently different from other medical procedures, because no other procedure involves the purposeful termination of a potential life.[7]

5. Hence, the states may adopt, consistent with the Constitution, a pro-life perspective in their legislative schemes for financing abortions.

6. If legislators may be prolife, may not other state officials, including judges, also be prolife when they are placed in the position of making the actual abortion decision, particularly for advanced gestation babies? I would argue that they can.

This argument has never been tested in court, but many associates of mine, including fellow judges and attorneys, feel it has merit.

I only wish I had this understanding of the law on October

19, 1982. It might have been the "creative alternative" to permit me even Supreme Court authority to acknowledge the interests of the unborn child in my decision. But, on reflection, I must conclude that I did my best in the hours before that fateful hearing.

On March 27, 1983, after a full morning of hearings on various cases, my hearing coordinator Deb Kammer and secretary-court recorder Marilyn King said, "We've got something for you." They laid on my desk a letter from the Tenure Commission.

My heart began to pound as I removed the letter (previously read by both staff members). They attempted to look sad, but I could already see the gleam in their eyes.

Sure enough, the one-page letter gave the answer I had been waiting for: the charges against me were dismissed with a private gentle admonition to be careful in the future. Praise the Lord! I was off the hook!

FOUR

Life Is in God's Hands

A FEW WEEKS BEFORE the Tenure Commission cleared me, I received the sad news that Jane Doe gave birth to her child, a seven-pound boy, but that he developed severe complications and died a few hours later. The valiant efforts of medical personnel were unable to save him.

The child initially appeared normal and healthy and there had been no complications in the pregnancy, labor, or delivery. But the boy soon developed primary pulmonary hypertension, a condition which prevents sufficient blood from reaching the lungs.[1]

I was initially very upset when I heard the child died. I had foolishly allowed myself to think that the child would one day thank me for his life. In my imagination, I had pictured him visiting me in later years to express gratitude for saving him. But now I would not have that privilege.

As I considered my reactions to the boy's death, I realized that my secret desires had been self-centered. I acknowledged this prideful attitude and reminded myself that my ultimate service is to God, who alone deserves the glory.

I had to concede that the baby's death must be God's will. I wouldn't have done it that way, but I'm not God. He made this child and he can decide when the child should cease living on earth to take his abode in heaven. Certainly from a human perspective there were many uncertainties about where and how this child would be raised had he lived.

Some people might cynically say: "The child's death proves that it would have been right for Jane to have had the abortion earlier to get the 'problem' over with sooner." I totally disagree.

The fact that someone will die does not justify killing him in advance. All of us are "terminal patients": death is just a matter of time for each of us (barring the Lord's return, of course). Does the fact that all of us will die give anyone the right to shorten a life by even one minute? Of course not—such would be murder.

Also, Jane Doe does not have to go through life with the guilt of knowing she caused her son's death.

In praying about the child's death a few days after hearing the news, I visualized the baby boy in heaven talking to his Creator. The Lord was telling the boy about the circumstances of his arrival and how a judge in Grand Rapids was willing to risk his judicial career to allow the child to live at least a few hours on earth rather than being brutally destroyed.

In my mind, I envisioned the child reflecting on this information for a moment and then saying, "Take care of that man, Father."

And God answered back, without hesitation, "I will, my child."

FIVE

The Facts and Morality of Abortion

What Abortion Is

While medicine is not my area of specialty, the essential medical facts about abortion are quite easy to understand. Killing living creatures is a concept even young children can readily grasp.

Put most simply, abortion is the deliberate and forcible termination of a woman's pregnancy with the consequent destruction of the unborn child.

To some, merely this definition is enough for them to know that abortion is wrong. Others, however, want to know more. They want to know when life begins and what physical and emotional effects abortion has on the three parties to the abortion: the mother, the unborn child, and the medical personnel. Let us look at these issues.

When does human life begin? At birth? At conception? Or somewhere in between?

Later, we will see the legal answer the Supreme Court ultimately gave to this question. But let's answer it now from a medical perspective.

For many hundreds of years prior to the late nineteenth century, most people in Europe and America believed that life entered the unborn's body at "quickening," the point in the fourth or fifth month of pregnancy when the mother can begin to feel movementsof her child.[1]

By 1857, however, the medical community had learned that "quickening" is a medically irrelevant time in pregnancy; the child actually moves in the womb long before this can be felt by the mother—certainly as early as two months after conception.[2]

In 1867, the New York State Medical Society passed a resolution asserting that:

> . . . from the first moment of conception, there is a living creature in process of development to full maturity . . . and . . . any . . . interruption to this living process always results in the destruction of life . . .[3]

As a result of this more informed perspective of when life begins, forty states soon passed new laws or they strengthened existing anti-abortion laws in the United States.[4]

In recent years, our knowledge of human development in the womb has increased even more. And the more we learn, the more we must concede that human life begins at conception. To choose any other point would be purely arbitrary and ignore scientific facts.

In April of 1981, U.S. Senator John P. East of North Carolina conducted hearings on a Human Life Bill. Both pro-and anti-abortion expert witnesses appeared to address the single medical question: "When does human life begin?" Their testimony on this point was summarized by Dr. Sean O'Reilly, scientific advisor to the committee and Professor of Neurology and Director of the Neuro-Biology Research Training Program at George Washington University in Washington, D.C. He said this:

> [T]here is nothing in the entire phenomenon of the transmission of life that deserves more to be called an event, scientifically speaking, than does fertilization. It is the

> natural and scientific boundary at which a new and genetically unique human individual can be said to begin his existence. We conclude, therefore, that by objective and scientific criteria the individual human being is a person throughout his [or her] entire biological development from conception, which is synonomous with fertilization, to natural death, and that the protection of the Fourteenth Amendment [of the Constitution] extends to all such real live material persons. Any other conclusion would be arbitrary, unsupportable by scientific fact or rational argument, divorced from objective reality, and based on a particular ideology, philosophy or creed.[5]

The medical evidence supporting this conclusion is voluminous. I do not want to review it here, but let me at least summarize the medical facts on this issue that mean the most to me as a layman:

1. We all begin life as a unique single cell. Each person reading this page was once a single cell containing all the basic information that makes every person unique from all other humans in the past, present, and future. In that first cell is a one-of-a-kind DNA blueprint describing each of us in all of our individuality. Like a computer chip loaded with precious encoded data, that first cell describes what our hair, eye, and skin color will be, our tendency toward certain height and weight, the shape of our head, ears, nose, our bloodtype and even our unique fingerprints for each finger. Our DNA template is different from our mother's and our father's and everyone else's in the world who ever was and ever will be. Even "identical twins" have different DNA prescriptions resulting in special features including totally different fingerprints.

2. A fetus is truly alive. The fetus moves, swims, sucks, urinates, and responds to noises and other stimuli.

3. A fetus is distinctly human. He or she possesses the 46 chromosomes that distinguish humans from other animals.

Advances in neonatology offer conclusive proof that the creature in the womb is a human being.[6] Every time a very small premature baby is saved, as more are doing these days, we can see them grow like full term babies; the only difference is that the "preemies" haven't had the same running start as the "full-termers."[6]

4. Conception is the only logical place to draw a line between human life and nonlife. This is the only time when there is a significant *qualitative* change. All other changes of this independent organism are *quantitative* changes of degree rather than of substance. At no time other than at conception can you reply "yes" to the following question: "Is the being's condition yesterday significantly different from today?" As we move backwards in time from birth back to conception, we can never reach a point where we can objectively say the organism is non-living, non-human, or non-independent until we reach the time of conception.

Even many pro-abortionists now concede that life begins at conception. Former abortionist Bernard Nathanson, who once ran the largest abortion clinic in the world, is now actively opposed to abortion. His mind was changed by the medical evidence. He was forced to conclude that human life begins at conception and, therefore, it is homicide to purposefully kill such life.[7]

Not all abortionists are as honest as Nathanson. Many ignore the obvious facts for the sake of financial reward, like slave traders of the last century. Others consider it a worse crime to allow a child to come into the world "unwanted." They see themselves as "mercy killers" of what they know are human children.

Our conclusion? Medically, abortion involves a deliberate and forcible interruption of a woman's pregnancy with the consequent killing of her human, unborn child.

The Consequences of Abortion

Effects on the child. No one pays much attention to what the nightmarish process of abortion means to the child. While I don't want to inflame your emotions, I do want you to consider abortion from the child's point of view so you can be appropriately outraged at the evil it is.

One would hope that if abortionists must kill the unborn, at least they could do so as quickly and painlessly as possible.

Unfortunately, they don't.

Abortions during the first three months of pregnancy are typically performed by Suction Abortion or by Dilation and Curettage (D&C). In Suction Abortions, the woman's cervix is dilated and the unborn child removed with a suction machine which literally rips the fragile child's body apart in a modern-day "drawing and quartering." With curettage, the wall of the womb is scraped with a sharp curette, cutting the baby's body into pieces. The remains are deposited in a container.

Second trimester abortions are done by Dilation and Evacuation (D&E), Saline Injection, and Prostaglandin Abortions.

In the D&E method, the abortionist must first stretch the opening to the womb wide enough to get his instruments into it. Then he or she uses heavy forceps to crush the baby's head and rib cage and dismember the body (including decapitation) so that the parts are small enough for removal.

Saline Injection Abortions are performed by injecting a concentrated salt solution into the mother's uterus. The salt is ingested by the child, burning the child's tender skin and poisoning him. The mother delivers a dead child within one to two days.

Prostaglandin causes the mother to deliver the child prematurely. The child dies from trauma as he or she passes through the birth canal or from the shock of exposure to the outside world before he or she is strong enough to take it.

Pregnancies in their final or third trimester are terminated by means of hysterotomy or Ceasarean Section Abortions. The abortionist opens the mother's womb surgically and removes the child. The child is allowed to die due to neglect or occasionally by more direct actions.

Does the child feel pain in abortion? It is incontestable that unborn children respond to noises, voices, and other external stimuli. According to John T. Noonan, Jr., the unborn child is physically able to feel pain by the end of the second month of pregnancy.[8] Imagine being disrupted from a place of security and comfort by a sharp object flailing wildly around us to cut us apart. Certainly we would wish for the fatal blow soon to end the pain and terror. Abortions that involve cutting or suction take approximately ten minutes until all the carnage is complete.[9]

Even worse would be to have our calm, friendly environment suddenly flooded with a biting salt solution, burning our tender, developing skin and producing painful gastric problems. Pouring salt on raw flesh hurts terribly; the child's mother soon herself learns this fact if, by accident, some of the salt solution enters an area where she can feel pain. This torture-death of saline solution poisoning can take as long as *six hours* to kill the baby by stopping its heart.[10] Would we consider treating a dog this cruelly?

Finally, where prostaglandin is used or where the child is surgically removed by hysterotomy, the tiny baby comes into the world before his or her body is ready for the shock. This too is cruelly painful. The medical staff watches the child's life ebb away and then the body is discarded like a tumor or a wart.

Then there are abortions that "fail." By "fail," I mean that the babies are born weakened and weary but still living, gasping for breath, clinging to life. Dr. Willard Cates, the chief of abortion surveillance for the Center for Disease Control in Atlanta, estimates that 400 to 500 abortions per year "fail" and the children involved born alive.[11]

Then what to do?

Put yourself in the shoes of the doctor. He has been diligently working to get rid of this "problem" for his patient. All of a sudden he realizes that the child is not cooperating—he or she is not dying as planned but is struggling for life. Can a doctor in such a position reverse his course and begin to take efforts to preserve the life of his former victim? Few doctors are able to shift their mental and emotional gears so quickly, especially after they have probably already severely compromised the ability of the child to survive any length of time.

If these babies could be given immediate life support treatment, many of them would survive. Some do. But most die because the physician, embarrassed by his "failure" and concerned about civil and criminal liability, orders that no steps be taken to help the struggling child.

In a well-documented article on the subject in the *Philadelphia Inquirer* on August 2, 1981, authors Liz Jeffries and Rick Edmonds describe numerous instances in which physicians actually took steps deliberately to kill the babies who survived abortions. The following is only one pathetic example:

> July, 1979, Cedars-Sinai Medical Center, Los Angeles, California: Dr. Boyd Cooper delivered [through abortion procedures] an apparently stillborn infant, after having ended a problem pregnancy of 23 weeks. Half an hour later the baby made gasping attempts to breathe, but no efforts were made to resuscitate it because of its size (1 pound, 2 ounces) and the wishes of the parents. The baby was taken to a small utility room that was used, among other things, as an infant morgue. Told of the continuing gasping, Cooper instructed a nurse, "Leave the baby there—it will die." Twelve hours later, according to testimony of the nurse, Laura Van Arsdale, she returned to work and found the infant still in the closet, still gasping.
>
> Cooper then agreed to have the baby boy transferred to an intensive care unit, where he died four days later. A coroner's jury ruled the death "accidental" rather than natural but found nothing in Cooper's conduct to warrant criminal action.[12]

What I'd like to know is where this callousness toward living babies came from.

Effects on the Mother. Abortions—particularly those which interrupt their first pregnancies—can cause serious problems for subsequent pregnancies. In a study by gynecologist Stanislaw Z. Zembrych, M.D. entitled "Fertility Problems Following an Aborted First Pregnancy,"[13] Dr. Zembrych states that 48 percent of women who had their first pregnancies terminated by abortion experienced complications with subsequent pregnancies.[14] He said:

> The results seem to be telling; they confirm the observations of other authors, indicating the prevelence of sterility, spontaneous abortion, cervical insufficiency, and premature delivery in women who underwent a previous abortion.[15]

Even worse are the emotional consequences for women who have had abortions.

Embedded on my mind is a recent TV documentary on abortion in which the viewers actually witness a woman being aborted. I myself watched in horror and disbelief, half of me wanting to watch it and the other half of me wanting to walk away in revulsion. We could hear the woman crying as the vacuum pump whirred, sucking her live child out to oblivion.

After the deed was done, the social worker attending the woman asked her if she hurt anymore. The woman's answer, given with noticeable despondency, spoke volumes. "Not *physically,* " she said.

The social worker, accurately perceiving that the woman was emotionally aching from what had just happened, said, "It's all right to feel bad. You've just lost something."

This answer made me sick. How can we go on playing games with life and death and right and wrong and dismiss the consequences as mere emotionalism? The woman *did* lose something—part of her own soul. The world also lost a ray of sunshine in a one-of-a-kind child's smile, never to be seen.

Pro-abortionists aften argue that pregnancy threatens the emotional well-being of many women. However, Dr. Myre Sim, in a study entitled "Abortion and Psychiatry,"[16] concludes that suicides by pregnant women are *far fewer* than suicides by nonpregnant women of the same age per capita.[17] Pregnancy is not the curse that abortionists suggest it to be. Dr. Sim has also discovered that women who experience post-abortive psychosis have a much poorer prognosis for psychiatric recovery than women who deliver live children and suffer from postpartum psychosis.[18]

Emotional problems resulting form abortions are common and severe.

Caring people in Milwaukee, Wisconsin established the "Pregnancy Aftermath Helpline," a free hotline for women whose pregnancies ended with a loss of the child through abortion, miscarriage, or adoption. Of 220 women who called the Helpline with problems following abortions, 189 or 76 percent said their distress was related directly to their abortion. Their problems included guilt, anxiety, depression, uncontrollable crying, nightmares, marital problems, flashbacks, a sense of loss, and other serious difficulties.[19]

Many women who have had these common problems belong to a national organization called Women Exploited by Abortion (WEBA). Founded by Nancy Jo Mann of Des Moines, WEBA provides support for the growing number of women who have been truly exploited by abortion. There are now 10,000 members of the organization which was formed in 1982. Mrs. Mann says that her own abortion was the most devastating event in her life:

> My little girl struggled for an hour and a half as she choked, burned and died—this was absolutely violent, violent thrashing around. . . . I delivered her myself because the nurses didn't make it to the room in time. Her eyes were opening, she had a full head of hair—she was precious, but

> she was dead. I had to deal with the fact that she was thrown in the incinerator and burned with the rest of the garbage for the day.[20]

The next few years, Mrs. Mann went through a mental breakdown, was admitted to psychiatric hospitals, and had a hysterectomy.

She says the word "exploited" in the organization name is not extreme, "We've been taken advantage of, we've been used, deceived, lied to—they got our money and they got our babies and they left us empty."[21]

One young woman who previously had an abortion called me during the Jane Doe abortion case. She wanted to tell Jane that it was a mistake for Jane to get an abortion because the resulting guilt would be unbearable. The woman said that while her own abortion was performed years before, she was just beginning, with God's help, to forgive herself for causing the death of her child.

A letter to the editor of *Moody Monthly* in the September 1983 issue says a lot:

> I am 19 and I had an abortion when I was 15. I had wanted to keep my baby, but I was pressured by the father and social forces... I have suffered for it, as have my family and friends. I grieve for girls who are faced with this life-shattering decision. The whole abortion dilemma is a crime.

One can certainly feel compassion for these dear young women and millions of others like them. So many are led into this terrible trap by ignorance in a society that officially says that abortion is just another simple surgical procedure.

Effects on the Medical Personnel. Imagine the stress of spending forty or more hours per week killing human beings.

Medical staffs in abortion clinics experience many emotional and related difficulties. One article described some of these problems:

> [One] clinic, one of the largest in the Rocky Mountain states, specializes in the D&E (dilation and evacuation) method of second-trimester abortion, a procedure in which the fetus is cut from the womb in pieces. Hern and Corrigan reported that eight of the 15 staff members surveyed reported emotional problems. Two said they worried about the physicians' psychological well-being. Two reported horrifying dreams about fetuses, one of which involved the hiding of fetal parts so that other people would not see them.[22]

The article also quotes another physician, Dr. Julius Butler of the University of Minnesota Medical School: "We've had guys [performing abortions] drinking too much, taking drugs, even a suicide or two. There have been no studies I know of, of the problem, but the unwritten kind of statistics we see are alarming."[23]

There are probably physicians and nurses who can blithely kill unborn babies all day long year after year without any apparent emotional or psychiatric reaction. But what couple would want such a physician to deliver their child in a "regular" delivery?

I consider it a perversion of the term "medicine" to describe the work of abortionists. The dictionary refers to the practice of medicine as the "science and art of diagnosing, treating, curing, and preventing disease, relieving pain, and improving and preserving health."[24]

There is no way abortion can fall within this definition. No way at all.

The Scope of Abortion

Take every child aged nine or below in Ohio, Indiana, Illinois, Michigan, Wisconsin, New York, New Jersey and Pennsylvania. I mean *every* child aged nine and under in these states. Then, with knives and poison, kill all 11.1 million of them and you will still have killed one million *fewer* children than were liquidated through legal abortion in this country between 1973 and January 1, 1983.[25] Mind you, these are not insects or cows or dogs. We are talking about humans, unique creations of an infinite God, each created with his stamp of ownership.

Remember how we grieved as a nation for the seemingly senseless deaths of 56,555 brave men in the Vietnam War?[26] That many unborn American children are killed *every 14 days* —silently, without much more than gasps, in antiseptic "benevolent" abortion clinics and hospitals throughout this land.[26]

Every day approximately 4100 living, yet unborn children are poisoned or ripped to bits or just allowed to die because they are an inconvenience to their parents' "lifestyles." Nearly one of every three pregnancies now ends in abortion.[27] In the District of Columbia, the number of abortions actually *exceeds* the number of live births.[28]

Whenever I see groups of little children, I can't help but wonder about the faces of those who are *not* there because they were aborted. I notice how no two children that I can see are the same physically, emotionally, or mentally. Each is so precious in his or her own way. I can only speculate about what the missing faces would look like, about what the children would tell us if they were there to talk.

It's as if the world never had lilacs and we did not know what a lovely fragrance we were missing. Until we see God's creative beauty in the real world, our minds cannot possibly fathom what was in his infinite mind to do. Life without these children is like a symphony without the french horns: we are poorer for it.

How impoverished we are as a people not to have these thirteen million young people in our world today. Each is infinitely valuable as a unique creation of God. We will *never know* what we are missing.

SIX

What the Bible Says About Abortion

THE VAST MAJORITY OF AMERICANS endorse the principle that those who intentionally kill other humans ought to be punished. As we become aware of the medical facts surrounding abortion, therefore, we should logically conclude that abortion is inherently wrong and ought to be considered a crime.

Unfortunately, many people who are aware that abortion results in the killing of unborn children nonetheless continue to support abortion on demand. It can be disconcerting to see these people's brazen cockiness. We are tempted to think, "Maybe they know something we don't; maybe abortions are really OK."

We need to realize that since sin entered the human race, there have been evil men and women who will do anything for the right price.

Gangster-style "hit men" are willing to kill others for enough money. Male and female prostitutes will sell their bodies. Public servants will sell votes or court rulings for bribes. There have been slave traders who committed unbelievably cruel outrages against black people for substantial profits.

So don't let the gloating confidence of evil men and women

who merchandise in the blood of unborn babies cause you to retreat from the truth. Make no mistake: the intentional taking of the life of another (albeit small) human being is an act that society has the right and obligation to outlaw.

Beyond this, Christian people who consider the Bible to be God's revealed word have even more reason to consider abortion wrong. It violates God's absolute moral standards.

God's loving heart reaches out to all who are suffering and afflicted. In Psalm 72:12-14, David pictures God's merciful heart:

> For he will deliver the needy who cry out, the afflicted who have no one to help. He will take pity on the weak and the needy and save the needy from death. He will rescue them from oppression and violence, for precious is their blood in his sight.

God not only cares for the downtrodden; he brings his judgment to bear on the nation which permits injustice. Such certainly was true of his people in Jerusalem before they were taken into captivity. While there were many reasons for the Jews' punishment, their cruelty and injustice was certainly one reason. The following verses from Ezekiel 22 express God's outrage. Verses 2-4:

> Son of man . . . will you judge this city of bloodshed? Then confront her with all her detestable practices and say: "This is what the Sovereign Lord says: O city that brings on herself doom by shedding blood in her midst and defiles herself by making idols."

Verses 6-7:

> See how each of the princes of Israel who are in you uses his power to shed blood. In you they have treated father and

> mother with contempt; in you they have oppressed the alien and mistreated the fatherless and the widow.

Verse 12:

> In you men accept bribes to shed blood . . .

Verse 27:

> Her officials within her are like wolves tearing their prey; they shed blood and kill people to make unjust gain.

Verse 29:

> The people of the land practice extortion and commit robbery; they oppress the poor and needy and mistreat the alien, denying them justice.

God condemns those who take advantage of the weak who cannot protect themselves. Evil men and women believe God does not see their sin, but the one who sees a sparrow fall cannot miss seeing the killing of the little ones created in his image.

Chapter 22 of Ezekiel ends with a challenge applicable to twentieth century America. Having detailed the injustices in Jerusalem, God again displays his heart's desire:

> I looked for a man among them who would build up the wall and stand before me in the gap on behalf of the land so I would not have to destroy it, but I found none. So I will pour out my wrath on them and consume them with my fiery anger, bringing down on their own heads all they have done, declares the Sovereign Lord. (Ezek 22:30-31)

Will you take your place to build up the wall and stand in the gap before God on behalf of America to restore justice to the unborn so God will not destroy us? The wall of justice and righteousness must be repaired. Judgment inevitably awaits if we do not act.

This biblical injunction to show mercy to the weak is not confined to the Old Testament. Jesus said: "Blessed are the merciful, for they will be shown mercy" (Mt 5:7).

Jesus illustrated this concept in the parable of the Good Samaritan. He also exemplified it in his own merciful death for sinful men who were powerless to help themselves.

The Apostle James endorses this same concept in James 1:27:

> Religion that God our Father accepts as pure and faultless is this: to look after orphans and widows in their distress and to keep oneself from being polluted by the world.

We American Christians who desire to obey God must do more than simply cluck our tongues with displeasure at the injustice and human carnage that goes on around us. We must be willing to do acts of mercy for those who suffer at the hands of the merciless. Proverbs 31:8-9 expresses it well:

> Speak up for those who cannot speak for themselves, for the rights of all who are destitute. Speak up and judge fairly; defend the rights of the poor and needy.

To apply these injunctions to abortion, we must know that human life begins at conception. Medical science proves this. It turns out the Bible also supports this medical conclusion.

David's prayer in Psalm 139:13-16 makes it clear that God himself forms children in the womb:

> For you created my inmost being; you knit me together in my mother's womb. I praise you because I am fearfully and wonderfully made; your works are wonderful, I know that

> full well. My frame was not hidden from you when I was made in the secret place. When I was woven together in the depths of the earth, your eyes saw my unformed body.

These verses beautifully describe the miracle whereby in nine short months a child grows from a speck smaller than a grain of sand to a baby in all its beautiful complexity, with its miles of veins and nerves, with eyes and fingerprints, a liver and eardrums. Yet no human finger has touched this marvelous creation. What a miracle!

Note that David in Psalm 139 uses the personal pronouns "I" and "my"—even when his body was being "woven" but still was "unformed." David also speaks of himself at the point of conception in Psalm 51:5, "I have been a sinner from birth, sinful from the time my mother conceived me."

In a similar vein, look at God's statement to young prophet Jeremiah:

> Before I formed you in the womb I knew you, before you were born I set you apart; I appointed you as a prophet to the nations (Jer 1:5).

God formed Jeremiah in the womb. He was in God's mind even *before* conception.

Job concluded that he should treat his servants with justice because:

> Did not he who made me in the womb make them [the servants]? Did not the same one form us both within our mothers? (Job 31:15)

In this age of science, organ transplants, and "test-tube babies," we think rather mechanistically about human functions. Let's keep it straight: *God* makes people in the womb; he imparts to them an immortal soul and stamps them with his image.

In the New Testament, we read of angel Gabriel's statement to Mary about her relative Elizabeth's pregnancy:

> Even Elizabeth your relative is going to have a child in her old age, and she who was said to be barren is in her sixth month. (Lk 1:36)

God's angelic messenger refers to the "sixth month" of pregnancy, implying that it is merely one stage in a progression from conception to birth.

After hearing this news, Mary hurried to Elizabeth's home and greeted her relative. What do we read then?

> When Elizabeth heard Mary's greeting, the baby leaped in her womb, and Elizabeth was filled with the Holy Spirit. (Lk 1:41)

At least three people were present: the two women and a *baby*, who "leaped" in her womb.

I think this unborn baby John was being filled with the Holy Spirit at this moment when Mary and the very small unborn baby Jesus appeared. Indeed, in Luke 1:15 the angelic prophecy about John the Baptist says, "He will be filled with and controlled by the Holy Spirit, even in and from his mother's womb." (Amplified Bible). Also we read that when the baby leaped in her womb, Elizabeth was filled with the Spirit. She tells Mary that: "As soon as the sound of your greeting reached my ears, the baby in my womb leaped *for joy*." (Lk 1:44)

We know from this statement that the baby and the mother are two independent persons and the baby had an emotion called *joy* at being in the presence of the mother of the Savior of the world and of Jesus himself.

However, God's most powerful statement that unborn children are really people is found in the incarnation itself. If God himself can take on the form of a tiny unborn child, that little being must be greater and more important than we can even begin to fathom.

Some may argue that God didn't take on human form until the unborn in Mary's womb was fairly well advanced. This position is both medically and biblically unsupportable.

In Matthew 1:18 we read:

> Mary was pledged to be married to Joseph, but before they came together, she was found to be with child through the Holy Spirit.

Mary's pregnancy was caused by the Holy Spirit of God. We are not told specifically how this happened, but it is clear she carried the Son of God in her womb from the beginning of her pregnancy.

Many in today's society would have counseled young, unmarried, pregnant teenager Mary to get an abortion. What if she had? Think of the loss to the world. And we sinful humans would never know what we were missing as we stampeded our way to hell without a Savior.

None of the thirteen million children "legally" aborted in this nation since 1973 are nearly as essential to the human race as is Jesus, but each one is nonetheless made in God's image and is uniquely created by God for God's own purpose.

These thirteen million innocents are not merely one mass of humanity, but are unique individuals who will never share their special hearts with us. And we will never know what we have lost as a people.

Before closing this chapter, let me quickly respond to two questions occasionally asked by Christians.

The first is an interpretation of Exodus 21:22 which some feel supports a pro-abortion position. This verse reads:

> If men who are fighting hit a pregnant woman and she gives birth prematurely but there is no serious injury, the offender must be fined whatever the woman's husband

> demands and the court allows. But if there is serious injury, you are to take life for life, eye for eye, tooth for tooth, hand for hand, foot for foot, burn for burn, wound for wound, bruise for bruise.

Some translations of the Bible say the woman had a "miscarriage" as a result of the fighting. If so, it would appear that the death of the child is inconsequential and that our only real concern is for the mother's well being.

The scholars who translated the NIV Bible, however, believe the real meaning of the verse is that the child is prematurely born alive and that the court is to consider whether *either* the mother *or* the child was injured. This translation is consistent with Keil and Delitzsch's respected commentary on the Old Testament. They state:

> If no injury was done to either the woman or the child that was born, a pecuniary compensation was to be paid. . . . The plural is employed for the purpose of speaking indefinitely because there might possibly be more than one child in the womb. "But if injury occur [to the mother or the child], thou shalt give soul for soul, eye for eye, . . ." Thus perfect retribution was to be made.[1]

The other question I have occasionally heard in Christian circles is, "Isn't it better for us to abort children? At least they will all go to heaven."

I've heard this question actually verbalized only a few times, but I sense that many Christians aren't overly concerned about the sin of abortion because this thought is in the backs of their minds.

I consider this argument to be preposterous. Where would such thinking lead? It could be used to justify killing born babies and young children who are under the "age of accountability." Perhaps we should have Christian "heaven sender" squads travelling from house to house to dispatch babies to the bliss of heaven. And why should Christian pediatricians work so hard to save the children of non-Christians if death is a better alternative?

Ridiculous? Of course.

God doesn't need us to kill defenseless children to obtain eternal life for them. He has already chosen his own and can be trusted to impart faith to them which, when exercised, will certainly result in their salvation.

Let's not forget that God alone, not man, has the right to give and to take life. It is our duty to obey God on earth which includes obeying the clear injunction, "Thou shalt not kill" (Exodus 20:13).

This includes people of all ages. Let God be God; let us be his people.

SEVEN

The Arguments for Abortion

DESPITE THE MEDICAL EVIDENCE and biblical interpretation each independently establishing incontestably the inherent wrongfulness of abortion, we often hear a number of arguments which attempt to justify the legality of abortion under certain circumstances. Before we go further, let us respond to these arguments.

Shouldn't a Woman Have the Right To Control Her Own Body?

This is the paramount pro-abortion argument of many groups, particularly of activist feminist groups.

Two basic points need to be made in responding to this argument. First, no one—man or woman—has the unqualified right to the control over his or her own body. For example, a person may legally be punished for taking or using an illicit or nonprescribed drug with his or her body. A person who unsuccessfully attempts suicide can be punished. A woman is not legally free to sell her sexual services even to a consenting adult man.

These are only a few examples of legal restraints on how we

use our bodies. There is *no* absolute right to control our bodies as we wish.

Second, medical facts show that abortion involves the deliberate taking of *another* person's life. The unborn child is not part of its mother's body, but is an independent person. We can consider a woman's right not to be pregnant. But we must also consider the child's right not to be killed. Between the pregnant woman who may suffer discomfort and inconvenience for nine months and the child who will die with abortion, it's quite clear that the child's right for life must far outweigh the mother's "right" to end her pregnancy a few months early.

Government Should Not Legislate Morality

Probably the most straightforward answer to this argument is, "Hogwash, we do it all the time."

All laws are a reflection of a philosophy of what is right and wrong.

In some cultures it's acceptable to kill and eat your victim. Rape is often committed with impunity when invading armies ravage a country and its inhabitants.

In some cultures, a man may kill or otherwise abuse his wife and children since they are considered his property. When we outlaw these practices in America, are we not in fact legislating an American brand of morality?

In 1857, the U.S. Supreme Court ruled that black slaves were the property of their masters.[1] We fought a Civil War over this question. The court's ruling was later overturned by constitutional amendments which could also be considered "legislating morality."[2]

Laws proscribing drug abuse by adults and laws against homosexuality by consenting adults *all* reflect their moral bases.

So, by necessity, we coercively "legislate morality" in our

laws. Why not do it with the leading form of child abuse in our nation today: abortion, the deliberate killing of unborn human babies?

A Woman Should Have the Freedom of Choice

"Don't impose the state's power in this essentially private issue between a woman, her own conscience, and her physician," we are told. "If abortion is wrong, let the woman bear the moral consequences herself."

The same argument could be used to justify infanticide, or any homicide for that matter.

The essential argument is: Don't make certain actions illegal; simply let people "do their own thing" and let them bear any natural or moral consequences that may follow their actions.

Another aspect of this argument is the idea that we shouldn't prosecute a woman for having obtained an illegal abortion because the deed is already done. It's as though we are closing the barn door after the horses have run away. What good does it do to punish the woman after her baby is dead? The baby can't be brought back to life again by punishing the mother or the doctor.

This argument misunderstands the purpose and function of our criminal justice system. We punish offenders to pay them back for their wrong and also to deter others from doing the same thing.

Punishing a murderer does not resurrect the victim, but justice accrues to society when those who commit murder are appropriately punished.

Abortion is *not* a private act any more than child abuse is. It violates another person's rights. Society has a legitimate *duty* to protect those who need protection. I am not being a "nosy neighbor" to be outraged when a fellow citizen kills his or her child before or after birth.

I am sickened by politicians who say, "I'm personally opposed to abortion, but I favor the woman's freedom of choice." This is a shell game. If you are really opposed to something, you will favor steps to have it eliminated, even if it involves the coercive power of the state. Imagine someone saying, "I'm personally opposed to child abuse, but I favor the parents' freedom of choice."

The argument is ludicrous. Don't fall for it.

No Child Should Be Unwanted. Such a Child Is Likely To Be Abused.

The scourge of the twentieth century, we are constantly told, is "unwanted babies." Almost as bad are "unplanned pregnancies." Who thought up this idea anyhow? What is an unwanted baby? Unwanted by whom? If you can somehow find them, are these babies less created in God's image than the "wanted" variety? Are they less alive? Do they have less innate potential? Of course not.

I sat next to a woman at a banquet recently. She told me that if abortion were legal when her mother was pregnant with her, she (the woman) would have entered the world prematurely and been summarily placed in some abortionist's refuse bucket for disposal elsewhere.

However, she was born before abortion was "legalized" in 1973, much to the chagrin of her mother. She was truly unwanted and inconvenient.

But her status as "unwanted" has ultimately changed. All of her siblings died, leaving her the sole living child of her mother. And through her, her mother became the grandmother of *twelve* grandchildren!

Sorrow has turned to joy. Despair has turned to rejoicing in that family.

So I ask again, what is an unwanted child? Do we mean unwanted when the mother is pregnant, or when the child is newborn? Or when the child turns two or a teenager? Doesn't every parent at weak moments wish his children lived elsewhere?

But, just for the sake of argument, assume a child is born with a label around his or her neck that he or she really is "unwanted." Then what?

In our country alone, it is estimated that there are 100 couples longing to adopt a white baby for every available child.[3] While the demand for non-white children is not quite that strong, they are wanted too. We do not have orphanages in America these days because they are not needed.

One of the most joyful tasks I have as a juvenile court judge is to preside over adoption cases. How thankful these couples are to hold their new children in their arms!

Many couples wait five years or more for a child to be placed in their homes. Why? Because we are killing "unwanted" children at the rate of 4100 per day, 1.5 million per year, through abortion.

Without question, no child would actually be "unwanted" if allowed to be born.

Finally, the argument implies that child abuse results from parents having to deal with children they don't want. The fact is that reported child abuse has gone up significantly since 1973 when abortion was "legalized."[4] While there are many reasons for this, it is abundantly clear that abortion has not reduced child abuse at all. In fact, in my opinion, the mentality of abortion tends to *increase* child abuse. If we can butcher kids legally before birth, it can't be so bad to do the same after a child is born. If my child misbehaves to the point of aggravation, I can think to myself: "Why didn't I abort this child when I had the chance."

Abortion has cheapened all of life.

We Need To Legalize Abortion or Else Women Will Obtain Abortions in Back Alleys With Coat Hangers

This same argument would support legalizing other forms of crime and vice.

For example, since some men will inevitably take drugs regardless of the law, let's at least make sure they not hurt themselves with bad "stuff" and let's oust organized crime from the business as well. How? Have the government license drug companies to dispense "approved" heroin and other drugs for a moderate fee. Obviously Medicaid would cover the cost of "prescriptions" for indigent junkies.

On child abuse. Some parents get hurt when their larger children retaliate after being abused by the parents. Since child abuse occurs even though laws outlaw it, we ought to legalize child abuse and have professional child abusers who will, for a fee, abuse a child for the parents without any danger of the child striking back at the parents.

Absurd? Of course. Government ought never to be in the business of doing or encouraging that which is harmful to its citizens.

Underlying this argument is the fallacious notion that illegal behavior must stop completely, or else the law must be repealed because it is "ineffective."

This premise is obviously invalid. Despite laws against murder, drug abuse, robbery and rape, people still unfortunately do these things. But the laws against these crimes serve the useful purpose of punishing wrongdoers, deterring potential offenders, and telling society what is right and what is wrong.

Apart from this philisophical argument, there is pragmatic evidence that legalizing abortion has not succeeded in substantially reducing the number of maternal deaths due to "back alley" abortions.[5] Also the total number of abortions, back alley and "legal," have increased dramatically since 1973.[6] Hence, the total deaths caused by "legalizing" the crime has greatly mushroomed. The "cure" is worse than the disease.

Parents Should Be Able To Abort a "Defective" Unborn Child To Spare Themselves and the Child a Lifetime of Pain and Expense

In these modern times, perhaps the only thing worse than an "unwanted child" is a "defective child."

The very concept of "defective" implies that children are supposed to be born accompanied by a written guarantee of physical, mental and emotional perfection.

As Christians, we know that there are no mistakes with God. God can use a special (a much more accurate term than defective) child in our lives for his purpose. Where have we gotten this foolish notion that life is supposed to be all easy, fun, and painless? We cannot grow up without a few trials along the way to produce in us true character.

The most appropriate people to respond to this argument are those courageous parents who themselves have had special children. The following were published as letters to the editor of our local newspaper:

> We are the parents of two retarded children. One has Down's Syndrome. There are no more giving, joyful, happy or precious children than Down's children. They are a genuine gift from God. Our son *teaches* us the meaning of patience and love and faith—just by his very existence. He has touched the lives of so many of our relatives and friends, adding a dimension they had not known existed. And he has helped us grow as a couple and as parents.

Another mother wrote:

> I. . . gave birth to a severely retarded child. Even though I would not have chosen Joey 12 years ago, today I love him as my special son. I would not choose to have any of my "normal" children severely handicapped. . . Should my parents have aborted me because years later I was to give birth to a retarded child? What I wish to emphasize is that God's way is not always our way. If we chose only that which appeared important or undemanding, I doubt if much would be accomplished or much love would be radiated in our lives. If not for my retarded son, I would not be defending the handicapped. Perhaps that's his purpose for life. I don't believe any life, regardless of its potential, is in

> vain. Most handicapped persons don't have a problem of being handicapped; their problem is society's acceptance of them and their handicap. . .

Finally, lest you think these are flukes, one more from a mother:

> Three years ago we had a child with Down's Syndrome, a closed esophagus and leukemia. After months of heartache, long hours at the hospital, not to mention unpaid bills, today he is the greatest joy of our lives. Anyone whose mischief can make me laugh before I've had my first cup of coffee in the morning can't be all bad. . .Who is more severely handicapped, someone who asks for nothing but hugs and cookies, or the person who would deny him an existence becuase he will never be a doctor or a lawyer?

Need I say more?

But what about parents who refuse to view their special child through the creative eyes of faith that God can give? Are these parents justified in killing their child? Of course not. Let them give the child up for adoption. These special children are *very* adoptable by couples, many of whom do see life from God's perspective.

Killing is a very short-sighted "solution" to a personal or societal "problem." Hitler used it in an attempt to rid his country of "defective"people and Jews. He killed many millions, but Germany became a land in which even the survivors' lives were cheapened.

A Woman Who Becomes Pregnant Through Rape or Incest Should Be Entitled to an Abortion

Many people who are otherwise anti-abortion are willing to concede that abortion is justified when pregnancy results from rape or incest.

One can visualize the 12-year-old girl who becomes pregnant by intercourse with her father or the older woman who is gang-raped and conceives a child. Each of these pregnant females has already been victimized by one or more brutal men; is it fair to victimize them again by requiring them to go through the pain and embarassment of bearing and raising truly unwanted children? If abortion could ever be justified, it would seem to be in this area.

But when you look closer at the real issues, I believe this argument is likewise unpersuasive.

To begin with, there are statistically few pregnancies that result from sexual assaults. According to Professor Basile Uddo, law professor at Loyola School of Law in New Orleans, there is only a 1 in 200 chance of a woman becoming pregnant for any single forcible sexual assault that results in intercourse.[7] It is theorized that pregnancy is rare because the trauma prevents ovulation, but physicians do not know for sure.

As far as incest is concerned, of 1500 families being treated for incest in Santa Clara County, California, less than 1 percent of them experienced a pregnancy, even though incest typically involves intercourse on a regular basis over a period of months or years.[8] This data is consistent with the observations of professionals elsewhere. Doctors are frankly baffled by the extremely low pregnancy rates in incest cases, but it seems to be a fact.

Despite the low numbers, it actually begs the real question simply to say that the problem occurs infrequently. In fact, it is accurate to say that *some* victims of sexual assault *do* become pregnant. Should they receive abortions?

As a juvenile court judge, I have seen many (too many) instances of child sexual abuse or incest. How wonderful it would be if a simple surgical procedure could erase all the problems from an incest victim's mind and emotions. Unfortunately, her real deep-seated problem is the *emotional* pain that her father and mother have betrayed her trust by using her for their own selfish needs instead of protecting her. Many victims begin regular sexual relations with their fathers long before they learn that it is wrong. When the girls turn 11 or 12, they learn from their friends that what their fathers have been doing is warped. Often the mother knows what is happening and does nothing to stop the abuse. Her motivation is to keep her family together at all costs.

To really solve the problem, the family needs intensive counseling and group therapy for a substantial length of time. If this is not done, the girl will typically engage in self-destructive behavior like incorrigibility, drug abuse, promiscuity, and suicide attempts. In later years, the girl will tend to marry men who will sexually abuse their children.

Based on data from Minneapolis, approximately 75 percent of teenage prostitutes were themselves prior victims of sexual abuse.[9] A similar number of teenage drug addicts were prior victims of sexual abuse.[10]

The problem does not seem to fade away with the years either. I know of groups of grown women who were sexually abused when they were young who now meet together for mutual support as they try to cope with the pain of the past.

On the other hand, where counseling and group therapy brings the father to the point of accepting responsibility for his abuse, learning why he did what he did (in most instances, *he also* was the victim of sex abuse as a child), and seeking the child's forgiveness, I have seen a significant measure of emotional improvement for the child.

However, to suggest that killing the pregnant girl's unborn child will somehow resolve her problems completely misses the mark. Expelling the child from her womb will not even begin to heal the girl's traumatized emotions.

In fact, abortion may well cause more problems for the girl, both emotionally and physically. Fathers involved in incest often encourage their daughters to abort to hide the evidence of his crime. Most girls do not voluntarily report incest; such families often hide their "secret." And, of course, the baby can be placed for adoption if the situation requires.

Similarly, the adult woman who becomes pregnant through a forcible rape would love an easy solution to her emotional and physical trauma.

We all want a solution. We Americans are enthralled with pushbutton, instant answers for our problems. If we feel ill, we take a pill. If we are hungry, we go to a fast food restaurant. If we are bored, we turn on some inane TV program. In a similar way, but far more seriously, if we have been raped and become pregnant, we would like to think we can solve the problem by destroying that "monster-child."

If only it were that easy. In all rape, it's the emotional hurt and the memories that are the worst. An awful crime has been committed and we want *something* to be done *now*!

So why not "terminate the pregnancy?"

Abortion won't heal the emotions, and now there is another totally innocent person to consider. As much as we naturally want to take revenge on someone, the rape is definitely *not* the unborn child's fault. So why inflict "capital punishment" on the child conceived in a rape to pay for the crime of the rapist? Two wrongs do not make a right.

Sure, this asks a lot of the woman. But many women in this position have courageously given birth to their children and either raised the children themselves or given them up for adoption. I have met young women who, with the help of caring Christians, are accepting the babies conceived by rape. At least they don't have to carry their babies' deaths on their consciences. Christian singer Ethel Waters was conceived when her mother was raped. Yet she has helped remind us all that, "His eye is on the sparrow and I know He watches me."

Nancy Jo Mann, the founder of Women Exploited by Abortion, says she knows two women in her organization who were brutally beaten and raped and subsequently chose abortions. Mrs. Mann says both are in "psychological counseling for the abortion—not the rape."[11]

Just as couples can grow in godly character by raising

"special" children, so a woman can, if unchangeable circumstances require, allow a painful, distressing experience to be the means of her growth.

As the mother of the Down's child said, "It is not easy, but who promised that life was to be easy?"

We Need Abortion Because the World Is Becoming Overpopulated

Who says the world is overpopulated? The media has so "hyped" this issue in recent years that we all pretty much take the overpopulation theory for granted.

We shouldn't. The fact is that there is plenty of space, food, water, and resources for billions more people on this globe.

Let's start with the issue of *space*. Assuming a world population of five billion (it actually is less than this) and giving each man, woman, and child in the world 1400 square feet (the size of a typical home) on which to reside, we would need seven trillion square feet to hold the world's population. How large an area is this?

Each square mile contains 27,878,400 square feet.

Therefore, to give each person 1400 square feet would require 251,130 square miles, an area less than the 262,134 square miles in the state of Texas.

In other words, the entire world's population could fit with some degree of comfort into the state of Texas with not one other person anywhere else in the world!

The world itself has 57,280,000 square miles of land (excluding, of course, oceans and lakes).[12]

If we literally filled up the world with people, each taking 1400 square feet, we could fit 1.14 trillion people in the world, more than 200 times our present world population. Despite how it feels waiting for a ride at Disney World or on a crowded subway in New York, we are far from being elbow-to-elbow in the world now or in the forseeable future.

We often equate crowded conditions and poverty. But they do not necessarily go together.

Japan, with a population density of 798 people per square mile, has a much higher Gross National Product (GNP) per capita ($4,450) than India which has only 511 people per square mile and a GNP per capita of only $140. West Germany, with its high standard of living, has a high population density of 636 people per square mile. China actually has a fairly low population density of only 232 people per square mile, but with a relatively low standard of living.[13] This makes me wonder why China has such stringent birth control and pro-abortion programs.

The United States has only 60 people per square mile.[14] The world as a whole has a population density of only seventy-seven people per square mile. Yet we hear so much that we're running out of room on this planet. It's time we heard some *real* facts.

As far as food is concerned, for centuries there have been occasional famines in parts of the world, even when populations were much lower. For example, probably the worst situation of "overpopulation" in North American occurred when less than 300,000 Indians lived here before white settlers came.[15] The Indians experienced consistent problems with starvation and famine. With the white man's arrival, both population and food production grew dramatically.

Jacqueline R. Kasun, an economist, cites an authority who concludes that "if all farms were to use the best methods now in use, enough food could be raised to provide an American-type diet for 35,100,000,000 people, almost ten times as many as now exist."[16]

The overpopulation boom is itself a myth. The numbers of children born to women in their child-bearing years has been declining consistently since 1800 with only brief "baby-boom" times interrupting the overall downward trend.[17]

If every female today decided to have no children, we would be only one generation away from extinction as a human race. It is equally true if we do not produce enough children to replace those aging and dying, the result is merely a delayed extinction of the human race.

Our media has failed to tell us that American women have been bearing *below* replacement level numbers of children *every year since 1972*.[18] Our population continues to climb only because of the momentum caused by the large group of post war "baby boom" children entering their childbearing ages. But they are producing fewer children per family than families in previous generations produced, too few to allow the population to do other than decline in subsequent years.

Our national leaders are concerned about both the prospect of a declining U. S. population (as already has occurred in some European countries) and the average median age of our people increasing significantly.[19]

If our present population trends continue, as early as 1990 there will be 25% fewer Americans available for military service than we had in 1970.[20] In fifty years, there will be only three persons of working age (15-64) to support those sixty-five and older. Today we have six.[21]

Projections of future population are remarkably sensitive to the "fertility rate" — the numbers of children born to an average woman in her fertile years. For example, if each woman has an average of 1.8 children (the current rate in the U. S.), and assuming no immigration from other countries, our population in the year 2080 (about 100 years) will be 201.6 million (an 8 percent decline from our present level of 220 million.)

However, if every woman has 2.2 children on the average, the population in 2080 will be 341.3 million, 69 percent more than produced by a fertility rate of 1.8.If we assume an annual immigration of 500,000 people, the population in 2080 for 1.8 and 2.2 fertility rates would be 268 million and 425 million respectively.

Clearly, the individual decisions of many couples has a profound impact on the future of our society. How can our prognosticators make even a reasoned guess on the future fertility practices of our people? The honest analysts will acknowledge their shortcomings.

Listen to one expert: "it is possible to speculate about future U. S. population size using very reasonable assumptions about future fertility rates and immigration. . . and be ***wrong by several hundred million.*** (emphasis in original).[22]

Prior projections of population growth even as recently as 1971 have already been totally discredited. The authors of the *Population Bulletin* acknowledge one big demographic surprise:

> In 1971, the Bureau of the Census issued four projections of births for the 1970's, ranging from 40.1 to 49.3 million. Actual births for the decade proved to be only 33.2 million, 17 percent below the lowest projection, and 23 percent below the lowest widely accepted series. Deferred marriage and childbearing and increased abortion all contributed to produce this result.[23]

The Census Bureau in 1971 could not forsee the impact of society's growing antipathy toward bearing children and even outright vengeance against children through abortion.

While we have focused on the population trends in the U. S., the fertility rates worldwide are likewise plummeting.[24] People around the world are seeking easy ways to prevent the "burden" of children. Yet by so doing, they ignore the future of the human race.

In any event, there is absolutely no reason that unborn children should be slaughtered by the millions in America because of some remote, catastrophic doom that *could* happen if a thousand uncertain contingencies occur, including our God taking his protective hand away from the creation he loved so much that he sent his Son to die for it.

EIGHT

The Power of Judicial Review

WHY DO WE HAVE "legalized" abortion in this country?

Most of us know that abortion became "legal" through a Supreme Court decision in 1973. But many people are a bit fuzzy on the details.

For a person to be prepared to do something about this horrendous blight, we need a brief lesson in basic constitutional law.

The U. S. Constitution, written by our founding fathers and adopted in 1789, is the fundamental, undergirding law of our country. Any statute passed by the U. S. Congress or a state legislature that contradicts the provisions of the Constitution should be considered invalid.

Any branch of government can determine whether a law violates the Constitution, but we have come to look primarily to the judicial branch to make these judgments. This power of courts to rule on the constitutionality of statutes is called the power of "judicial review."

Courts do not rule on laws in the abstract. They rule on real cases involving real people. To challenge the constitutionality of a law, someone must bring a case before a court. Where statutes are controversial, it is not difficult to find people willing to file lawsuits, to challenge the laws. The American Civil Liberties Union (ACLU) has been particularly successful in finding people to file lawsuits and then in getting courts to declare laws and executive decisions unconstitutional.

The power of judicial review is found nowhere in the Constitution. It was not formally established in a real case before the U.S. Supreme Court until 1803 when Chief Justice John Marshall wrote the opinion in the case of ***Marbury* v *Madison*.**[1] The statute under review in ***Marbury*** was a law passed by Congress giving the Supreme Court the authority to act as a trial court to order a governmental official to do what his job requires of him.[2]

The problem was that the Constitution seemed to withhold such power from the Supreme Court. The Constitution said one thing. The law passed by Congress said the opposite. What should the Supreme Court do?

Chief Justice Marshall framed the issue this way: "[W]hether an act repugnant to the Constitution can become the law of the land." With eloquence, Marshall answered this question in the negative. He concluded that a "law repugnant to the Constitution is void," and that "[i]t is emphatically the province and duty of the judicial department to say what the law is." Where there is a conflict between two laws, courts are to decide the matter. Judges cannot support unconstitutional laws; to do so violates their oaths of office to enforce the law "agreeably to the Constitution and the laws of the United States."

Since the clear words of the Constitution would not permit the Supreme Court to do what Congress attempted to mandate, Justice Marshall and the rest of the Supreme Court ruled that the statute was unconstitutional and void.

This is how judicial review should work. Any ordinary citizen can read the opinion and say, "The Justices were right. They told the Congress to follow the Constitution."

Judicial review gives the court the "last word." But it is

absolutely essential to understand that the judiciary has this authority not because it is more powerful than the other two branches of government but because it is the servant of the Constitution, as all branches of government should be. The Court's role in judicial review is merely to reaffirm to the other governmental branches that the people's intentions as expressed in their Constitution are more important than any law the Congress may pass or any action taken by the Executive branch.

A government publication entitled "The Supreme Court of the United States" says this about the Court's function:

> [Alexander] Hamilton had written that by invalidating unconstitutional legislation the Court would be ensuring that *the will of the whole people,* as expressed in their Constitution, would be supreme over *the will of a legislature,* whose statutes might express only the temporary will of part of the people.[3] (emphasis in original.)

Indeed, this is what Hamilton said about the Court in his *Federalist Papers* which he helped to write in the 1780s to convince the colonial legislatures to adopt the Constitution. Hamilton's *Federalist* No. 78 contains a number of interesting insights about the proper role of the judiciary in the eyes of the framers of our Constitution:

> No legislative act, therefore, contrary to the Constitution, can be valid.[4]
>
> The interpretation of the laws is the proper and peculiar province of the courts. A constitution is in fact, and must be regarded by the judges as, a fundamental law. It therefore belongs to them to ascertain its meaning as well as the meaning of any particular act proceeding from the legislative body. If there should happen to be an *irreconcilable*

variance between the two. . . , the Constitution ought to be preferred to the statute, the intention of the people [preferred over] the intention of their agents.[5]

This theory of judicial review sounds reasonable, but the following quotes will demonstrate that while Hamilton may have been a superb statesman, he was a myopic prophet:

> The judiciary, from the nature of its functions, will always be the least dangerous to the political rights of the Constitution.
>
> The judiciary . . . has no influence over either the sword or the purse; no direction either of the strength or of the wealth of the society, and can take no active resolution whatever. It may truly be said to have neither FORCE NOR WILL but merely judgment.
>
> The simple view of the matter . . . proves incontestably that the judiciary is beyond comparison the weakest of the three departments of power; that it can never attack with success either of the other two. . . It equally proves that though individual oppression may now and then proceed from the courts of justice, the general liberty of the people can ***never*** be endangered from that quarter; I mean so long as the judiciary remains truly distinct from both the legislature and the executive. For I agree that "there is no liberty if the power of judging be not separated from the legislative and executive powers."[6] (emphasis supplied.)

Hamilton's last statement — that liberty depends on a judiciary separated from the other branches — is profoundly true. Whenever the judiciary assumes the function of the other branches of government and exerts both force and will, liberty gives way to tyranny. This is what has happened in our country in recent years.

While most Americans have heard of the *Federalist Papers*, few know about the *Antifederalist Papers*, written by a number of men who vigorously *opposed* the adoption of the Constitution. In responding to Hamilton's arguments about the judiciary, two of the authors of the *Antifederalist Papers*, Thomas Treadwell and Judge Robert Yates, proved to be much better predictors of the future than Hamilton.

The original *Antifederalist Papers* were published in the spring of 1788 in the *New York Journal*, one year before the Constitution was adopted. They make for interesting reading. The following are some selected quotes:

Consider the following quote:

> The Supreme Court under this Constitution would be exalted above all other power in the government, and subject to no control... I question whether the world ever saw, in any period of it, a court of justice invested with such immense powers, and yet placed in a situation so little responsible.
>
> There is no power above [the judges], to control any of their decisions. There is no authority that can remove them, and they cannot be controlled by the laws of the legislature. In short, they are independent of the people, of the legislature, and of every power under heaven. Men placed in this situation will generally soon feel themselves independent of heaven itself.[7]

The authors of the *Antifederalist Papers* continue their argument by predicting that:

1. The judiciary will become the final arbiter of the letter and spirit of the Constitution, and that its legal opinions will carry the force of law.

2. The judiciary will eventually subvert the powers of the states and enlarge the federal government's authority.

3. The judiciary will tend to greatly expand its sphere of authority and power.

4. The judiciary will act to circumscribe the powers of the legislative branch.[8]

Finally, the *Antifederalist Papers* touch on an issue that we will be returning to later in this book:

> A constitution is a compact of a people with their rulers; if the rulers break the compact, the people have a right and ought to remove them and do themselves justice. . . [W]hen this power is lodged in the hands of men independent of the people, and of their representatives, and who are not constitutionally accountable for their opinions, no way is left to control them but ***with a high hand and an outstretched arm.***[9] (emphasis in original.)

As we shall see, the Supreme Court has gone well beyond these dire predictions by absorbing legislative and executive governmental powers and ignoring the written law. Liberty and the rule of law have been largely replaced with a form of tyranny and the rule of men.

While the authors of the *Antifederalist Papers* were remarkably accurate in their predictions of modern day judicial activism, I believe they were wrong to claim that judicial activism was the *intent* of the framers of our Constitution, or even that such activism is consistent with a fair interpretation of the Constitution. They knew human nature well enough to predict the tendency of our courts to usurp legislative and executive authority, but they were wrong to suggest the Constitution encourages this result.

The Constitution gives the judicial branch "judicial power" as contrasted with legislative or executive power.[10] There is a significant distinction between these governmental functions, a distinction known for thousands of years. In Isaiah 33:22 we read: "for the Lord is our *judge*; the Lord is is our *lawgiver*; the Lord is our *King*" (emphasis added).

It is one thing for a perfect and loving God to reign supreme in all these governmental functions. But when fallible men on earth have authority, we desire that these three functions be divided with checks and balances to keep each limited in power and ultimately subservient to the people.

The judicial power given to the courts by the Constitution is the power to decide specific cases based on existing law. In the American system, courts do not have the inherent power to make laws nor to amend the Constitution by their decisions. When they violate these principles, do not judges in fact violate their oaths of office whereby they have pledged to "support *this* Constitution?"

To further buttress my position that the dire predictions of the *Antifederalist* authors were not intended by the Constitution, we can look to legal scholars who have written on the subject of judicial review. One of the greatest scholars in this area was Michigan's most distinguished jurist, Justice Thomas M. Cooley (1824-1898) of the Michigan Supreme Court.

In his landmark text, *Constitutional Limitations*, Justice Cooley explains his view of a court's proper role in construing a constitution and determining the constitutionality of a statute.[11] Justice Cooley based his perspectives on his own analysis of the Constitution as well as on court decisions he studied in writing his well-researched treatise.

If we understand some of Cooley's basic arguments about how judicial review should work, we can better evaluate the way it is actually being done today. I think you will agree that Cooley's principles of judicial review are eminently reasonable and approach the subject with intellectual honesty.

The following is a summary of Cooley's scholarly perspectives:

The first step of judicial review is for a court to determine what the Constitution means. To do this, judges should observe the following principles:

1. Determine what the words of the Constitution meant when they were written:

> A court or legislature which should allow a change of public sentiment to influence it in giving to a written Constitution a construction not warranted by the intention of its founders, would be justly chargeable with reckless disregard of official oath and public duty.
>
> The meaning of the Constitution is fixed when it is adopted and it is not different at any subsequent time when a court has occasion to pass on it.[10]

2. Determine the intention of the framers from the plain words of the Constitution itself.

> Possible or even probable meanings, when one is plainly declared in the instrument itself, the courts are not at liberty to search for elsewhere.[11]

3. Look at the entire Constitution and each provision in its context to determine the true intention of each part.[12]

4. Where there are apparent conflicts between various provisions of the Constitution, give preference to a construction of it which will "render every word operative rather than one which may make some words idle and [of no effect.][13]

5. "In interpreting clauses, we must presume that words have been employed in their natural and ordinary meaning."[14]

6. Read the Constitution in the light of the common law of England and the Declaration of Independence.[15]

7. Where, by using the above steps, there are still doubts or unexplained ambiguities as to the meaning of a provision, then and only then may a court use other means of determining the issue. The primary method is to contemplate:

> . . . the object to be accomplished or the mischief designed to be remedied or guarded against by the clause in which the ambiguity is met with. . . Great caution should always be observed in the application of this rule to particular given

cases; that is, we ought always to be certain that we do know, and have actually ascertained, the true and only reason which induced the act.[16]

Cooley warned that judges should declare statutes unconstitutional with great reluctance and hesitation:

> It must be evident to anyone that the power to declare a legislative enactment void is one which the judge, conscious of the fallibility of the human judgment, will shrink from exercising in any case where he can conscientiously and with due regard to duty and official oath decline the responsibility. The legislative and judicial are co-ordinate departments of the government, of equal dignity; each is alike supreme in the exercise of its proper functions. . .[17]

But sometimes courts must exercise judicial review. Since declaring a statute unconstitutional is a grave step (the equivalent of saying that the legislature has disregarded Constitutional limitations), courts should properly observe the following principles in passing judgment on suspect statutes:

1. Rule on a case only when all justices of a particular court are present. Don't decide such a case with a bare quorum.[18]

2. Don't pass on a Constitutional question in a case unless to do so is necessary to the determination of the cause. Said Cooley:

> "While courts cannot shun the discussion of constitutional questions when fairly presented, they will not go out of their way to find such topics."[19]

3. Don't listen to the argument for the unconstitutionality of a statute by a party whose rights are not affected by the statute and, therefore, who has no real interest in the outcome.

"The statute is assumed to be valid, until someone complains whose rights it invades."[20]

4. A court may not declare a statute unconstitutional and void solely on the ground that a provision of a statute is unjust or oppressive or because it supposedly violates the natural, social or political rights of a citizen or group, *unless* it can be shown that such injustice is prohibited or such rights are protected or guaranteed by the Constitution.[21]

In researching cases for this point, Cooley found that most courts supported his position. However, he found at least one court decision that seemed to base its decision on "fundamental principles" other than those found in the Constitution. His response is illuminating:

> [T]here would. . .be [a] very great probability of unpleasant and dangerous conflict of authority, if the courts were to deny validity to legislative action on subjects within their control on the assumption that the legislature had disregarded justice or sound policy. The moment a court ventures to substitute its own judgment for that of the legislature, in any case where the Constitution has vested the legislature with power over the subject, that moment it enters into a field where it is impossible to set limits to its authority, and where its discretion alone will measure the extent of its interference.[22]
>
> The courts are not the guardians of the rights of the people to the State, except as those rights are secured by some constitutional provision which comes within the judical cognizance. The protection against unwise or oppressive legislation, within constitutional bounds, is by an appeal to the justice and patriotism of the representatives of the people. If this fail, the people in their sovereign capacity can correct the evil, but courts cannot assume their rights. The judiciary can only arrest the execution of a statute when it conflicts with the Constitution.[23]

A footnote to this quoted section cites an opinion of U. S. Supreme Court Chief Justice White in *McCray* v *United States*

> [N]o instance is afforded. . . where [a statute enacted within the rightful powers of the legislature] was declared to be repugnant to the Constitution, because it appeared to the judicial mind that the particular exertion of constitutional power was either unwise or unjust. To announce such a principle would amount to declaring that, in our constitutional system, the judiciary was not only charged with the duty of upholding the Constitution, but also with the responsibility of correcting every possible abuse arising from the exercise by the other departments of their conceded authority. So to hold would be to overthrow the entire distinction between the legislative, judicial, and executive departments of the government, upon which our system is founded, and would be a mere act of judicial usurpation.[24]

5. Neither can courts declare statutes void because the statutes seem to violate fundamental principles of republican government unless, of course, the Constitution specifically declares such out of bounds.[25]

6. Neither can courts declare a statute void because the statute seems to violate the "spirit" of the Constitution but which is not expressed in words or at least mandated by necessary implication.

> . . . [I]t is only in express constitutional provisions, limiting legislative power and controlling the temporary will of the majority, by a permanent and paramount law, settled by the deliberate wisdom of the nation, that I can find a safe and solid ground for the authority of courts of justice to declare void any legislative enactment. Any assumption of authority beyond this would be to place in

> the hands of the judiciary powers too great and too undefined either for its own security or the protection of private rights.[26]

A footnote in this section of Cooley's book contains an articulate and relevant quote by a Judge Black from Pennsylvania:

> If we [the judiciary] can add to the reserved rights of the people [through an inappropriately broadened interpretation of the Constitution], we can take them away; if we can mend, we can mar. If we can remove the landmarks which we find established, we can obliterate them. If we can change the Constitution in any particular, there is nothing but our own will to prevent us from demolishing it entirely. The great powers given to the legislature are liable to be abused. But. . . there is no shadow of reason for supposing that the mere abuse of power was meant to be corrected by the judiciary.[27]

7. Never declare a statute unconstitutional and void unless the invalidity of the act is established beyond a reasonable doubt — the same burden in finding a person guilty of a crime with which he is accused.[28]

> The opposition between the Constitution and the law should be such that the judge feels a clear and strong conviction of their incompatibility with each other.[29]

If you have absorbed even some of this chapter, you know more about the proper method of judicial review than most graduates of law schools. In fact, many judges now sitting on the benches of our courts are largely unaware of these reasonable principles.

Since the turn of the century, a growing number of judges have marched to the alluring drumbeat of judicial activism in which judges assume the role of the legislative and the executive branches — all in the guise of interpreting the Constitution. As a result, the judiciary now wields seemingly limitless power.

In the next chapter we shall see how judicial activism and usurpation led relentlessly to the audacious decision in *Roe* v *Wade* in 1973.

NINE

The Growth of Judicial Legislation

WHILE THE POTENTIAL for judicial excess has existed since the founding of our nation, the Supreme Court demonstrated commendable self-restraint until the early 1900's when, very gradually, its decisions began to reflect the justices' personal beliefs more than the actual meaning of the words of the Constitution. This trend reached a crescendo in *Roe* v *Wade*, the 1973 case "legalizing" abortion.

Most legal scholars agree that the activist trend began with the case of *Lochner* v *New York* (1905),[1] in which the Supreme Court struck down as unconstitutional a New York law restricting bakery employees from working more than 60 hours per week or 10 hours in any day. The Court held the law to be an "illegal intereference [of government] with the rights of individuals. . .to make contracts." This may sound authoritative, but no actual provision of the Constitution requires this conclusion.

We may personally agree or disagree with the wisdom of such a law. But the real question is: *who* has the authority to say this law is invalid? Courts have *no* authority to strike a law down unless it violates a specific constitutional provision. Otherwise, the power to make or rescind laws is the sole responsibility of the legislature whose members are directly accountable to the people.

Between 1905, when the *Lochner* case was decided, and 1938, a majority of the Supreme Court declared numerous laws unconstitutional in the same dubious manner.[2]

Eventually, however, the membership of the Supreme Court sufficiently changed that the minority view of the Court became its new majority. In the 1938 opinion of *Erie Railroad Company* v *Tomkins*, this new majority called the Court's past approach to decisions "an unconstitutional assumption of power by courts of the United States which no lapse of time or respectable array of opinion should make us hesitate to correct."[3]

It must be stressed, however, that those opinions which were later called "unconstitutional" nonetheless possessed the force of law when they were decided.

Unfortunately, the Court's self-reform did not last too long. One significant decision was *Cooper* v *Aaron* in 1958.[4] Prior to *Cooper*, the Court's rulings were said to directly impact only the parties before the Court while affecting other potential litigants only indirectly. According to George Washington University Law Professors Arthur Selwyn Miller and Jerome A. Barron, beginning with *Cooper*,

> the Court has sought to expand the operative impact of its decisions to cover more and more people. Choosing their cases because of the general importance of the issues, rather than because of the litigants, they have become a third legislative chamber in fact.[5]

This expanded impact, along with the Supreme Court's tendency to base decisions on what it considers to be "wise" or "fair" rather than on the actual words of the Constitution, has resulted in many of our laws being judicially modified or revoked. The process has accelerated as lower courts have followed the lead of the Supreme Court.

As a result, we have seen questionable decisions relating to criminal justice procedure, capital punishment, pornography regulation, freedom of speech, freedom of religious exercise and many other areas. In these cases, the Supreme Court and lower courts have made legislative-type decisions of general impact based on the judges' subjective impressions of what is wise, desirable, or fair regardless of the actual language of the Constitution.

A classic example of such a decision is the famous *Miranda* case.[6] In *Miranda*, the Supreme Court issued general rules for all police agencies to use in interrogating a crime suspect who is in custody. Neither party before the Court in *Miranda* asked that a general policy be issued, but the Court created one nonetheless.

We may agree or disagree with the *Miranda* rules, which require the police to advise suspects of their right to remain silent, that anything they say may be used against them, that they have the right for an attorney before and during any interrogation, and that an attorney will be appointed for them at no expense before any questioning if they desire. The question, however, is whether a court deciding a case between two litigants should enact a law which is binding on all police agencies and all courts in the country and which is based on a highly subjective reading of the Constitution.

Justice White, dissenting in *Miranda*, said,

> The Court's holding today is neither compelled or even strongly suggested by the language of the Fifth Amendment, is at odds with American and English legal history, . . .involves a departure from a long line of precedent [and] underscore[s] the obvious — that the Court has not discovered or found the law in making today's decision, nor has it derived it from some irrefutable sources; what it has done is to make new law and new public policy in much the same way that it has done in the course of interpreting other great clauses of the Constitution.

The majority of the Court was not interpreting the written law of the Constitution. The justices simply created their decision out of whole cloth. Perhaps this process is tolerable in many cases. Perhaps judicial legislation by five of nine unelected men (and now one woman) on the Court who are appointed for life as final arbiters with no right to appeal is reluctantly acceptable in many areas of law. Perhaps most citizens would agree that most of the "laws" the Court has "passed" in this way are not overly objectionable.

But that is not the point. Remember the insightful words of Judge Black of Pennsylvania quoted in the last chapter: "If we [the judiciary] can add to the reserved rights of the people, we can take them away; if we can mend, we can mar."

We pay a large price when we allow the Supreme Court to disregard the actual language and meaning of the Constitution in decisions we do not find particularly offensive. We open the door for decisions that permit the Court to work injustices against individuals — unborn children, crime victims, or practicing Christians—all in the solemn name of "constitutional law."

This principle can be demonstrated most clearly in the judically created right to privacy which culminated eventually in the right to abortion on demand.

There is no specific mention whatsoever in the Constitution of a right to privacy. On the other hand, who doesn't like their privacy? Arguing against it is like trying to argue against motherhood, ice cream, and apple pie. But who wants a small, unelected group of citizens, from whom there is no right to appeal, defining this right of privacy for all of us with no regard whatsoever to written law? I, for one, don't want to give that kind of authority to such a small group of fallible people.

But the Court exercised such authority in 1965 when it decided *Griswold* v *Connecticut*[7]. In *Griswold* the Supreme Court reviewed a state law in Connecticut making it a crime for a person to dispense contraceptive devices. Mr. Griswold was convicted of this offense and fined $100. His appeal led ultimately to the Supreme Court.

Those not schooled in the law would be amazed at the methods a court can use supposedly to justify striking down a statute as unconstitutional. The court can overturn a statute becuase the Court feels the statute is "unconstitutionally vague," or because it violates "due process" considerations of "fundamental fairness," or for a host of other legal sounding reasons. Often the Court uses such language simply to make it appear that a decision is based on established legal absolutes rather than what it is truly based on: the subjective feelings of a majority of the justices.

In writing the majority opinion in *Griswold*, Justice Douglas chose not to use one of the more traditional methods of striking down the Connecticut statute. Instead, he creatively fashioned a new constitutional right — the right of privacy.

In his opinion, Justice Douglas stated that:

> specific guarantees in the Bill of Rights have penumbras [partial shadows] formed by emanations from those guarantees that help give them life and substance.

The good Justice elsewhere explained that he is referring to the First, Third, Fourth, Fifth, and Ninth Amendments of the Constitution which, he opines, cast their "penumbras" in the same general direction. As we blink our eyes into focus, lo and behold: there appears the constitutionally protected right of privacy! One legal writer humorously stated that Justice Douglas:

> skipped through the Bill of Rights like a cheerleader — "Give me a P. . . give me and R. . .an I" and so on, and found P-R-I-V-A-C-Y as a derivative or penumbral right.[8]

Having discovered this hitherto unknown right of privacy, Douglas went on to conclude that the right protects couples who wish to use and purchase contraceptive devices. Hence the Connecticut law must fall to the more fundamental precepts of the Constitution.

I encourage the reader carefully to scrutinize the constitutional amendments cited by Douglas. See if you can find the mysterious penumbras Douglas found which require the voiding of a statute passed by the duly elected representatives of the State of Connecticut outlawing the distribution of contraceptives. We are not debating the relative wisdom of laws against contraceptives. The issue is whether the Constitution enacted in the late 1700's eliminates a state's authority over this issue in 1965. Is not considerable intellectual dishonesty involved in concluding that it does? In any event, certainly the action of the Court in *Griswold* violated many, if not all of the traditional rules of judicial review.

Justice Black, joined by Justice Stewart, wrote a scathing dissent in *Griswold*:

> I like my privacy as well as the next one, but I am nevertheless compelled to admit that government has a right to invade it unless prohibited by some specific Constitutional provision. . .
>
> I do not believe that we are granted power by the Due Process Clause [of the Fourteenth Amendment] or any other Constitutional provision or provisions to measure constitutionality by our belief that legislation is arbitrary, capricious or unreasonable, or accomplishes no justifiable purpose, or is offensive to our own notions of "civilized standards of conduct." Such an appraisal of the wisdom of legislation is an attribute of the power to make laws. . . a power which was specifically denied to federal courts by the convention that framed the Constitution. . .
>
> If these formulas [of judicial review] are to prevail, they require judges to determine what is or is not constitutional on the basis of their own appraisal of what laws are unwise or unnecessary. . . Surely it has to be admitted that no provision of the Constitution specifically gives such a

blanket power to courts to exercise a supervisory veto over the wisdom and value of legislative policies and to hold unconstitutional those laws which they believe to be unwise or dangerous.

Many Supreme Court opinions enacting such "judicial legislation" have been accompanied by vigorous dissents calling attention to the dishonesty which is occurring. But only lawyers or law students particularly interested in the subject will spend much time reading the dissents of most cases. A dissent, after all, is the statement of the losers.

Justice Black, while not always consistent, was a refreshing voice on the Court; he often stood for judicial restraint and a more strict construction (as opposed to a loose construction) of the Constitution. His voice has been sorely missed since his death in 1971.

In 1973, drawing heavily on concepts created in *Griswold*, the Supreme Court decided *Roe* v *Wade*,[9] the original, infamous abortion case.

Roe v *Wade* originated in Texas in March of 1970. A pregnant, unmarried woman using the ficticious name of "Jane Roe" brought suit against Henry Wade, the District Attorney of Dallas County. She asked the Federal District Court in Dallas to declare the Texas criminal abortion statute unconstitutional and to restrain the District Attorney from enforcing the statute which made abortion a crime.

Three judges of the Federal District Court in Dallas, hearing the case together, ruled in favor of Jane Roe's personal request for an abortion since they felt the Texas laws making abortion a crime unconstitutionally infringed on her Ninth Amendment rights. However, this lower Court refused to generally restrain the District Attorney from enforcing the state's abortion laws against others who wanted abortions.

Because she did not receive all she wanted, Miss Roe appealed the case ultimately to the Supreme Court. District

Attorney Henry Wade also appealed the part of the decision unfavorable to him. The Supreme Court issued its opinion in January of 1973, nearly three years after Jane Roe filed her original suit.

Justice Harry Blackmun will always be remembered as the justice who wrote the majority opinion in *Roe* v *Wade*. Six other justices either totally agreed with his analysis of the law or else filed concurring opinions. Two justices, Justice White and Justice Rehnquist, filed vigorous dissents.

Almost everyone was shocked by Justice Blackmun's 51-page majority opinion — some pleasantly shocked, and others devastatingly shocked. Even Jane Roe and her attorneys must have been amazed at the exceedingly wide scope of the decision. It essentially "legalized" abortion, not only for Jane Roe, not only for Dallas, not only for the State of Texas, but for the entire United States. Abortions were ruled "legal" under almost all circumstances for women who were at virtually any stage in their pregnancies, from conception to a minute before birth.

Justice Blackmun's opinion is filled with isolated arguments, each internally consistent, but virtually unrelated to the others and totally unattached to any real bedrock of substantive law or fundamental principles. The legal edicts in the Court's holding are themselves clear enough, but emanate seemingly from nowhere.

Justice Blackmun begins commendably by stating his goal:

> Our task, of course, is to resolve the issue [of abortion] by constitutional measurement, free of emotion and of predilection.

Having said this, Justice Blackmun, after ruling on procedural issues relating to who has standing to sue, examines the history of abortion in the world.

While the history of abortion may well be an interesting subject, it has *nothing* to do with the Supreme Court's proper function when evaluating the constitutionality of a statue. Even if Justice Blackmun found that *all* of our ancestors were bloodthirsty abortionists (which would be *far* from the truth), the Supreme Court would nonetheless have absolutely *no* authority to declare a state statute unconstitutional which outlaws abortion unless that statute specifically contradicted the Constitution. *That* is *the* issue.

Having dazzled us with his erudite but totally irrelevant history of abortion, Justice Blackmun explains why it is we have laws making abortion a crime. In other words, he probes the relative *wisdom* of having anti-abortion laws in the 1970's.

The *reasons* why states passed anti-abortion laws are also irrelevant to the actual issue at hand. Unless such laws violate a specific constitutional provision, state and federal legislatures have the untrammeled authority to pass laws unimpeded by our courts since legislatures are a separate and equal branch of government with *the* power to make laws.

I am tempted to "take on" Justice Blackmun in his many isolated arguments about the history of abortion and the purpose for anti-abortion legislation. However, since his arguments in these areas are completely irrelevant to the Supreme Court's proper role, I do not wish even to dignify them by responding. Indeed other authors more learned than myself have already impeccably refuted Blackmun's points.[10]

I do not want the reader to lose sight of the essential issue amidst the "red herrings" strewn about by Justice Blackmun in his opinion.

The real issue is whether the Constitution specifically prevents a state from passing a law making abortion a crime. At one point in his opinion, Justice Blackmun does briefly touch on this issue. He begins Section VIII of the ruling with an understatement: "The Constitution does not explicitly mention any right of privacy."

As we have already learned, this should end the discussion. But Justice Blackmun goes on:

> In a line of decisions, however,. . .the [Supreme] Court has recognized that a right of personal privacy. . . does exist under the Constitution.

Justice Blackmun then cites a number of prior cases, including *Griswold* v *Connecticut*, in which the Supreme Court created or at least mentioned the right to privacy in varying contexts.

Over the years, the Court has replaced the actual language of the Constitution with legal precedents. The Court has piled precedents one on top of another like a brick mason who builds a wall without a plumbline. As each level of bricks is added, the wall incrementally leans in one direction until the top layer isn't above the foundation at all. Few people would want to live in such a building.

After citing the cases about privacy, Justice Blackmun deftly unsheaths his gleaming weapon. Devoid of logical support from anything he has just said or will say, including the cases on privacy, Justice Blackmun simply pronounces *the law* by judicial fiat:

> This right of privacy, whether it be founded in the Fourteenth Amendment's concept of personal liberty and restrictions upon state action, as we feel it is, or, as the District Court determined, in the Ninth Amendment's reservation of rights to the people, is broad enough to encompass a woman's decision whether or not to terminate her pregnancy.

I cannot overemphasize how unsupported by its context is this bold, raw statement. And yet, without these words, which themselves are suspended in mid-air, nothing else in the opinion would ever produce the conclusion that American women can have abortion on demand. It's like having our serenity shattered by a bomb suddenly exploding behind our backs with bone-jarring force. Before the bomb explodes, everything is fine; after the explosion, our lives are forever changed.

Having used this bombshell to extend the nebulous right of privacy to the extreme of including a woman's decision to have an abortion, Justice Blackmun throws a sop to the anti-abortion side by stating that a woman's right to abortion is not totally absolute: the State has a growing right to oppose an abortion as the unborn child matures in his or her mother's womb (my words, not Justice Blackmun's.)

Without explaining any details, Justice Blackmun then explores the legal boundaries of the State's interest in opposing abortion.

Since the Fourteenth Amendment to the Constitution says that a state cannot deprive a *person* of life without due process of law, Justice Blackmun next addresses the issue of whether a fetus is a "person" within the language and meaning of the Fourteenth Amendment. His conclusion: "[T]he word 'person,' as used in the Fourteenth Amendment, does not include the unborn."

I fully agree with the many legal scholars who persuasively argue that Justice Blackmun was totally incorrect in this conclusion. However, as important as this personhood issue sounds, it is nonetheless a side issue. *Roe* v *Wade* does not turn on the question of whether an unborn child is a person in the terms of the Fourteenth Amendment. The decision hinges on the issue of whether the Court has any authority to do what it did.

The most bizarre part of Justice Blackmun's opinion involves his discussion on when life begins. He implies but never specifically states that if, as Texas had argued in the case, life begins at conception, the unborn's rights would then take precedence over the rights of their mothers to "terminate their pregnancies."

But he doesn't answer the question. While sounding very

authoritative and dogmatic in all other parts of his opinion, Justice Blackmun backs away from addressing the issue of when life begins:

> We need not resolve the difficult question of when life begins. When those trained in the respective disciplines of medicine, philosophy, and theology are unable to arrive at any consensus, the judiciary, at this point in the development of man's knowledge, is not in a position to speculate as to the answer.

So on one hand, Justice Blackmun dodges the issue of when life begins. But, on the other hand, he concludes that a woman can "legally" destroy her unborn child up until birth for virtually any reason. Thus we must logically conclude that Justice Blackmun, without saying so, ***did*** determine that life does ***not*** begin until birth, or else that the question of when life begins is truly irrelevant to him in his ultimate ruling. Either conclusion flies in the face of medical facts and ultimate justice.

Having made many disjointed and unrelated points, Justice Blackmun again, without any logical or causal link to support his position, issues his final pronouncements:

> A state criminal abortion statute. . . is violative of the Due Process Clause of the Fourteenth Amendment:
>
> (a) For the stage prior to approximately the end of the first trimester [first three months], the abortion decision and its effectuation must be left to the medical judgment of the pregnant woman's attending physician.
>
> (b) For the stage subsequent to approximately the end of the first trimester, the State, in promoting its interest in the health of the mother, may if it chooses, regulate the abortion procedure in ways that are reasonably related to maternal health.

(c) For the stage subsequent to viability [the stage set by the Court at 24 to 28 weeks of gestation where the child is potentially able to live outside the mother's womb, albeit with artificial aid], the State in promoting its interest in the potentiality of human life may, if it chooses, regulate, and even proscribe abortion except where it is necessary, in appropriate medical judgment, for the preservation of the life or health of the mother.

There you have it. Any state anti-abortion law which is more restrictive than these sweeping statements are immediately rendered void by the vote of seven men on the Supreme Court. This meant in 1973 that *every* state law was swept aside. While part (c) above suggests that a state may outlaw abortions after "viability," it cannot do so when abortions are necessary for the "preservation of the life or health of the mother." Since "health" can obviously include the mother's emotional health, abortion is legal up until the time of birth.[11]

The results of this infamy are history. 4100 unborn children per day are "legally" killed because the Supreme Court said that no one may interfere with the carnage. After all, it's the "law of the land!"

TEN

An Evaluation of *Roe* v *Wade*

IN THE PREVIOUS CHAPTER, I resisted the temptation to get baited by the spurious arguments generated by Justice Blackmun in his majority opinion in *Roe* v *Wade*.

For example, Blackmun's discussion of the history of abortion, while perhaps interesting, is totally irrelevant to the real issue, which is: what does the *Constitution* say about abortion? The Supreme Court has no authority to strike down laws unless the Constitution mandates such an action by actual language or by logical and reasonable interpretation.

Similarly, when Blackmun examines the motivations of state legislatures in enacting anti-abortion legislation, this again is *not* the proper role of a court unless that court needs to determine whether the legislature actually intended to frustrate a purpose explicitly created by the Constitution.

The only part of Justice Blackmun's opinion that *is* relevant to the proper constitutional role for the Supreme Court is where Blackmun appears to look at the Constitution and, upon doing so, concludes:

> This right of privacy, whether it be founded in the Fourteenth Amendment's concept of personal liberty and restrictions upon state action, as we feel it is or, as the District Court determined, in the Ninth Amendment's

> reservation of rights to the people, is broad enough to encompass a woman's decision whether or not to terminate her pregnancy.[1]

This sentence should send every American scurrying to his or her copy of the Constitution with the reasonable expectation of finding a provision like:

> No state may make abortion a crime since a woman has a constitutional right to terminate her pregnancy.

We might not expect to find language quite this explicit, but we certainly have the right to expect something close to it, since one co-equal branch of government is voiding the work of another co-equal branch ostensibly because the other has violated the basic law of the land—the Constitution.

According to Blackmun, the District Court based its decision in favor of abortion on the Ninth Amendment; the Supreme Court found its decision emanating from the Fourteenth. Let's look at both.

The Ninth Amendment reads:

> The enumeration in the Constitution, of certain rights, shall not be construed to deny or disparage others retained by the people.

What does this amendment, enacted in 1791, have even remotely to do with abortion or even childbirth?

Is the District Court suggesting that if an issue is not specifically mentioned in the Constitution as being a power of the state government, the people as individuals retain that power?

The Constitution does not specifically mention that states may outlaw child abuse, air pollution, drug abuse, prostitution or even homicide itself. Yet courts have consistently upheld the constitutionality of state laws making these actions crimes. So why is abortion a sacred cow?

Not even the Supreme Court agreed with the District Court's position that the right to abortion on demand arose from the Ninth Amendment. Instead, the majority of the Supreme Court ruled that the right emanates not from the Ninth but from the Fourteenth Amendment, passed in 1868.

The section of the Fourteenth Amendment of which Justice Blackmun speaks is the so called "due process" clause:

> [N]or shall any State deprive any person of life, liberty, or property without due process of law.

Again, we must ask: What in the world do these words even *remotely* have to do with a woman's right to kill her unborn offspring with impunity? Whether a lay person simply looks at the clear meaning of the words themselves, or whether a legal scholar performs an indepth study of all the historical and other contexts, we arrive at the same answer: The Fourteenth Amendment has absolutely nothing to do with the "right" to abortion.

According to Professor Raoul Berger of Harvard Law School in his masterful book *Government By Judiciary*, the Fourteenth Amendment was passed after the Civil War to enhance rights for Blacks.[2]

After a lengthy analysis of the history of the Fourteenth Amendment, Professor Berger concludes that the Amendment was enacted,

> to insure . . . that an oppressed race should have the "equal benefit of all laws for security of person and property as is enjoyed by white citizens." This was the purpose constitutionalized by the Fourteenth Amendment.[3]

In construing this amendment, it is helpful to realize that the Fifth Amendment, enacted in 1791, contains a similar phrase but without reference to a "State." The Fifth Amendment reads:

> . . .[N]or [shall any person] be deprived of life, liberty, or property, without due process of law.

Alexander Hamilton spoke about the meaning of these words in 1787:

> The words "due process" have a precise technical import, and are only applicable to the process and proceedings of the courts of justice; ***they can never be referred to an act of the legislature.***[4] (emphasis added).

Yet in *Roe* v *Wade* the Supreme Court used these words to sweep away anti-abortion acts of ***all*** states' legislatures in a manner totally inconsistent with the meaning of the words of the Constitution.

Another way to view *Roe* v *Wade* is to consider what Justice Cooley, author of *Constitutional Limitations*, would say about it from his scholarly perspective of how courts ***should*** construe the constitutionality of statutes. Since Cooley is no longer alive, we will have to make the assessment ourselves.

A quick look at Cooley's principles of constitutional construction shows convincingly that the Supreme Court in *Roe* v *Wade* violated most, if not all of his principles. Let's briefly document this assertion:

1. Cooley's Principle: A court should look to the meaning of the words as they were intended by the authors of the Constitution when written.

Roe* v *Wade: The Court made no serious attempt to apply the actual statements of the Constitution to the abortion issue. The Court's majority simply lifted individual words such as "liberty" out of context from the Constitution and gave these words arbitrary meanings. Justice Blackmun was at least candid enough to concede: "The Constitution does not explicitly mention any right of privacy" (from which the "right" of abortion springs.)

Clearly, those who wrote and voted for the Fourteenth Amendment in the 1860's had no desire whatsoever to use this amendment to strike down laws making abortion a crime.

In fact, Justice Rehnquist, in writing his dissent in *Roe* v *Wade*, pointed out that when the Fourteenth Amendment was passed, thirty-six states had laws limiting abortions altogether. Upon the passage of the Fourteenth Amendment in 1868, not one person, ***not one solitary person*** was quoted as saying, "Well, I guess we can't outlaw abortion any more."

2. Cooley's Principle: The intention of the framers (of the Constitution) is to be found in the plain words of the Constitution itself.

Roe* v *Wade: No regard whatsoever was given to the intent of the framers, but only to the intent of a majority of the Supreme Court in 1973.[5]

3. Cooley's Principle: Look at the entire Constitution and each provision in its context to determine the true intention of each part.

Roe* v *Wade: The Court did not cite one complete constitutional provision, much less engage in a scholarly attempt to discern the true intention of the Fourteenth Amendment by the context or other sections of the document. Just a glance at the preamble to the Constitution shows that the Founders were concerned for yet unborn future generations:

> "and secure the Blessings of Liberty to ourselves and our Posterity."

4. Cooley's Principle: In interpreting clauses, we must presume that words have been employed in their natural and ordinary meaning.

Roe* v *Wade: The Court gave meanings to words that were oblivious to, if not antithetical to, their ordinary meaning. For example, the phrase from the Fourteenth Amendment: "[N]or shall any State deprive any person of life, liberty, or property, without due process of law," has nothing to do with abortion rights or even childbirth. If anything, these words could be used to *support* anti-abortion legislation since you cannot deprive a person of "*life* . . . without due process of law." Yet the majority of the Supreme Court concluded that these words mean that a woman has the constitutionally protected right to kill her unborn offspring. This is ludicrous at best.

5. Cooley's Principle: Read the Constitution in the light of both the common law (from England) and the Declaration of Independence.

Roe* v *Wade: While Justice Blackmun attempted to describe the common law's view of abortion, his findings seemingly did not affect the outcome of his decision.

In the seventeenth and eighteenth centuries under the common law, our ancestors, with their unscientific view of when life begins, still made the killing of a "quickened" fetus a crime.[6] This common law rule itself was effectively declared unconstitutional by *Roe* v *Wade* along with all other anti-abortion laws.

If the Court spurned the common law, it outright defied the Declaration of Independence. In this foundational philosophical document, we read:

> We hold these truths to be self-evident, that all men are created equal, that they are endowed by their Creator with certain unalienable Rights, that among these are Life, Liberty and the pursuit of Happiness.

In other words, our rights come not from the State, not from the Supreme Court, but from our Creator. If this "unalienable" right to life has been given to all human creations of God, then no Court has the authority to take it away. Yet take it away they claimed to do in outright defiance of this revered document of our country.

6. Cooley's Principle: Judges should declare statutes unconstitutional with great reluctance and hesitation.

Roe* v *Wade: The Court showed no reluctance at all. It struck down anti-abortion laws with an almost gleeful exuberance. The Court went far beyond even the remedy requested by "Jane Roe."[7]

7. Cooley's Principle: A Court may not declare a statute unconstitutional and void solely on the ground that the provisions of the statute are unjust or oppressive or because it supposedly violates the natural, social or political rights of a citizen or group, unless it can be shown that such injustice is prohibited or such rights protected or guaranteed by the Constitution.

Roe* v *Wade: The Supreme Court generated the "right" to abortion out of thin air because a majority felt it was fair to do so, irrespective of the actual language of the Constitution.

8. Cooley's Principle: Never declare a statute unconstitutional and void unless the invalidity of the act is established beyond a reasonable doubt.

Roe* v *Wade: Has the Court convinced ***anyone*** that the Constitution really says what they said it does? Even some ***pro-abortion*** legal scholars feel *Roe* v *Wade* is legally inept as we will see. But I have not heard of a single anti-abortionist who has concluded that Justice Blackmun was essentially correct in *Roe* v *Wade.* The Supreme Court has not borne the burden of proof. The Justices act as though they don't need the support of the Constitution nor the concurrence of the citizenry in their decisions, but can essentially amend the Constitution as they please. I believe they are wrong. More on this in subsequent chapters.

Don't simply take my word that the Supreme Court has misread the Constitution. Many others have expressed themselves on the same subject.

Let's begin with President Ronald Reagan, head of the Executive Branch, who wrote an article in the Spring 1983 edition of the ***Human Life Review*** entitled "Abortion and the Conscience of the Nation.

In this well-written and powerful article, President Reagan says:

> Make no mistake, abortion-on-demand is not a right granted by the Constitution. No serious scholar, including

> one disposed to agree with the Court's result, has argued that the framers of the Constitution intended to create such a right. . . Nowhere do the plain words of the Constitution even hint at a "right" so sweeping as to permit abortion up to the time the child is ready to be born. Yet that is what the Court ruled [in *Roe* v *Wade.*][8]

Having heard from the head of the Executive Branch of government, let's consider the words of some legislators. Senator John P. East (R-N.C.) stated:

> Few Constitutional scholars argue. . . that the Supreme Court's holding in *Roe* v *Wade* (1973), striking down all fifty state anti-abortion laws, represents a correct reading of the Constitution.[9]

Senator Thomas F. Eagleton (D-Mo.) wrote that *Roe* v *Wade*: "Is not only a moral abomination, but [is] also a legal embarassment."[10]

Many other senators and congressmen have been equally vociferous in expressing their incredulity at *Roe* v *Wade*.

How about the Judicial Branch? While seven justices of the Supreme Court ruled in favor of the majority holding in *Roe*, two justices registered clear and eloquent dissents.

Justice White, in his dissent, said:

> The Court. . .simply fashions and announces a new constitutional right [and] with scarcely any reason or authority for its action, invests that right with sufficient substance to override most existing state abortion statutes. . .As an exercise of raw judicial power, the Court *perhaps* has authority [but] in my view its judgment is an improvident and extravagant exercise of the power of judicial review. . .[11] (emphasis added.)

Justice Rehnquist, in his dissent, stated:

> The decision here. . .partakes more of judicial legislation than it does of a determination of the intent of the drafters of the Fourteenth Amendment. . .To reach its result, the Court necessarily has had to find. . . a right that was apparently completely unknown to the drafters of the [Fourteenth] Amendment. . .There apparently was no question concerning the validity of [the Texas anti-abortion statute enacted in 1857] or of any of the other state statutes when the Fourteenth Amendment was adopted [in 1868]. The only conclusion possible from this history is that the drafters did not intend to have the Fourteenth Amendment withdraw from the States the power to legislate with respect to [abortion].[12]

Another federal judge, U. S. Circuit Judge Robert Bork, former Solicitor General, called *Roe* v *Wade* an "unconstitutional action by the Court" involving the "deformation of the Constitution."[13]

I have yet to find one legal scholar — pro or anti-abortion —argue that *Roe* v *Wade* flowed from either the spirit or the language of the Constitution.

Archibald Cox, noted former Watergate prosecutor, wrote in 1976 concerning *Roe* that, "The Justices read into the generality of the Due Process Clause of the Fourteenth Amendment a new 'fundamental right' not remotely suggested by the words [of the Constitution]."[14]

Stanford University School of Law Professor John Hart Ely makes it clear that he personally favors abortion on demand. However, as a constitutional scholar, Professor Ely has grave concerns about the Supreme Court's decision in *Roe* v *Wade*:

> [What] is frightening about *Roe* is that [its] super-protected right [for abortion] is not inferable from the language of the Constitution, the framers' thinking respecting the specific problem in issue, any general value derivable from the provisions they included, or the nation's governmental structure.

He calls *Roe* a "very bad decision" because it is "not Constitutional law and gives almost no sense of an obligation to try to be."[15]

Obviously sympathetic to abortion "rights," Bob Woodward and Scott Armstrong make some interesting comments about how *Roe* v *Wade* was written in *The Brethren*, their "behind the scenes" expose of the Supreme Court.

> The clerks in most chambers were surprised to see the justices, particularly Blackmun, so openly brokering their decision like a group of legislators. There was a certain reasonableness to the draft [opinion] some of them thought, but it derived more from medical and social policy than from Constitutional law. There was something ***embarassing*** and ***dishonest*** about this whole process. It left the Court claiming that the Constitution drew certain lines at trimesters and viability. The Court was going to make a medical policy and force it on the states. As a practical matter, it was not a bad solution. As a constitutional matter, it was ***absurd***. The draft was referred to by some clerks as "Harry's abortion."[16] (emphasis added.)

Arthur Selwyn Miller, George Washington University National Law Center Professor Emeritus and also a person sympathetic to abortion, expresses his amazement at *Roe* v *Wade*:

> Justice Blackmun's lengthy opinion gives few clues as to the reasoning from facts to conclusion; he neatly bridges the chasm by taking a mental leap. . .I do find it of more than passing puzzlement to dredge up sound reasons for the conclusion. . . [A]bortion is an idea whose time has come, something that seven justices recognized and then clothed their conclusion in the turgid language with which lawyers are familiar, language loaded with history and other data. Just how privacy became a part of liberty is really not explained; nor indeed are the criteria set forth by which the

> Court finds new rights, hitherto undiscovered, in the . . . prose of the Constitution. I applaud the decision; I find difficulty with the "reasoning.". . The growing recognition of a population problem. . . has now been translated into constitutional law. . . It took the anonymous Jane Roe and Mary Doe to translate their very personal and very human desires not to be mothers into a national policy against unwanted children, embedded now in the fundamental law, and thus to allow the Supreme Court to articulate a policy of voluntary population limitation in the name of privacy. . . The Supreme Court moves in mysterious ways its wonders to perform. Let me not carp at a long overdue decision; but do let me shake my head in bewilderment as to how one can make such a decision jibe with orthodox jurisprudence or judicial methodology.[17]

Finally allow me to quote from a guest editorial published in the *Wall Street Journal* by Terry Eastland, editor of the *Virginian Pilot*:

> *Roe* v *Wade* imposed on the nation a view of the abortion issue lacking constitutional warrant. . . A right to abortion obviously can't be found in the Constitution. Neither can it reasonably be concluded from a principled interpretation of the Constitution.[18]

I could continue quoting from numerous governmental leaders, attorneys and legal scholars in similar ways. But I believe I have made the point: The right to abortion did not come from the Constitution; it came from the personal inclinations of seven fallible public servants on the U. S. Supreme Court. They generated this right out of thin air and added "legalese" verbiage to make it sound authoritative.

The Supreme Court, with no right to appeal above it, legislated abortion on demand and forced this policy down the throats of 200 plus million Americans.

ELEVEN

The Legacy of *Roe* v *Wade*

BETWEEN 1973, when *Roe* v *Wade* was decided, and the present, the Supreme Court ruled on a number of abortion-related cases further clarifying "the law" relating to abortion rights.

Some of these decisions tended to reduce the scope of abortion and others expanded the scope. But the fundamental "right" to abortion on demand was not seriously challenged until a group of these cases was decided by the Court in June, 1983.

Some of us had hoped that the Court might use this opportunity to reverse itself and retreat from its absolutist, pro-abortion position in *Roe*. However, we were sorely disappointed.

This time Justice Lewis F. Powell, Jr. wrote the majority opinion in the 6 to 3 decision of the lead case *Akron* v *Akron Center for Reproductive Health*:

> [A]rguments continue to be made . . . that we erred in interpreting the Constitution [in *Roe* v *Wade*]. Nonetheless, the doctrine of *stare decisis*, while perhaps never entirely persuasive on a constitutional question, is a doctrine that demands respect in a society governed by the rule of law. We respect it today, and reaffirm *Roe* v *Wade*.[1]

Note that Justice Powell did not point us to sections of the Constitution which clearly give a woman the right to "terminate her pregnancy." Rather, he points back ten years before to that intellectually and legally indefensible opinion in *Roe* v *Wade*. He talks of the "rule of law"; he should have said the "rule of us men."

"Today," says Justice Powell, "we respect *stare decisis*." I'm glad he said "today," because on many days, the Supreme Court totally ignores the doctrine of *stare decisis* and reverses or ignores their own prior holdings.

Stare decisis is a Latin expression meaning a doctrine or policy of following rules or principles laid down in previous judicial decisions unless they contravene ordered principles of justice.

Stare decisis should not be used when concepts of justice require a different result — which they clearly do in this abortion issue.

Justice Powell's opinion in the *Akron* case contained another amazing statement. The law under scrutiny by the Supreme Court was an ordinance in the brave City of Akron, Ohio which required that women receive adequate factual information before they could legally have an abortion. One fact that had to be told to the women was "the unborn child is a human life from the moment of conception."

We know that this statement is a medical fact. Why did the Supreme Court's majority object to telling women the medical truth?

Justice Powell explained that the requirement to give women this statement is "inconsistent with the Court's holding in *Roe* v *Wade* that a State may not adopt one theory of when life begins to justify its regulation of abortions."

Note that he did not deny that human life begins at conception; he merely stated that you can't use this fact to regulate or outlaw abortion. In effect, Justice Powell is saying, "Don't confuse us with the facts, we've already made up our minds. Abortion is here to stay!"

On the more positive side, Justice Sandra Day O'Connor, appointed by President Reagan in 1982, voted against the *Akron* majority. The vote is now 6 to 3 instead of 7 to 2 as it was in 1973. Who can tell what a few more years will bring?

The next few years could bring a reversal of *Roe* v *Wade* and a judiciary that is more subservient to our written Constitution.

Or the future could bring worse evils than those we have already seen.

Even at the present time, as a direct outgrowth of the *Roe* v *Wade* mentality and an evolving sociological approach which tries to distinguish between "meaningful life" and "non-meaningful life," courts are giving parents increasing legal powers to kill their unwanted, "defective" children.

This certainly occurred in the infamous "Infant Doe" case in Bloomington, Indiana. In April, 1982, Infant Doe was born with a form of mental retardation, Down's Syndrome, and a defect which prevented him from eating. Distressed at having brought a "retarded" child into their lives, Infant Doe's parents refused to authorize the corrective surgery necessary for the child to eat properly. The child was given neither food nor water, and died of starvation and dehydration after six days of suffering.[2] The local court endorsed the parents' authority to pursue this planned homicide.

Furthermore, on appeal the Indiana Supreme Court refused to intervene to save the child. Several couples stepped forward and offered to adopt Infant Doe. But the parents refused. They chose the final and complete "solution"—death to the child.

This is not an isolated case. The Surgeon General of the United States, Dr. C. Everett Koop, says that many similar "Baby Doe" cases every year go unreported. I myself was confronted with an almost identical case a few years ago.

A local, upper-middle class couple was grieved when the wife gave birth to a Down's syndrome child with a physical malady similar to Infant Doe's. The parents preferred not to have corrective surgery performed. Their family physician had told them that such surgery was too experimental and would be an extraordinary attempt to save a "severely retarded" child.

However, specialists at our local neonatal intensive care unit were insistent that such surgery was fairly routine. But the parents did not want to hear this.

A doctor from the unit called me for guidance on the case. I simply looked at the Michigan Juvenile Code which considers it neglectful for the parents to "neglect or refuse to provide...medical [or] surgical...care necessary for [their child's] health."[3] It was, at least on the surface, a clear case of neglect. Pursuant to my authority in such cases, I ordered the surgery performed and Protective Services investigated the parents for neglect.

A preliminary court hearing was scheduled in the case. The ultimate result of the court's action could have been to place the child for adoption if the parents persisted in their neglectful attitudes and actions. Unfortunately, the child unexpectedly died after surgery and the case became moot.

In an attempt to ensure care for special children, the Reagan administration issued anti-infanticide regulations in March, 1983 for use by all hospitals.

These administrative rules required the posting of notices in hospitals reminding hospital staff that federal law prohibits the "discriminatory failure to feed and care for handicapped infants" in the hospital. The notice included a hotline number for nurses and others to use to report violations of the law.

The American Academy of Pediatrics challenged these regulations in a federal court in Washington, D. C. Judge Gerhard Gesell struck down the regulations as "arbitrary and capricious agency action."[4] Again, the Courts win over the executive branch. The Administration has since issued revised rules that include the formation of hospital committees to review cases. There is now a better chance to influence hospital policy to save these children.

Why is the law so cruel to those least able to help themselves? We seem to have learned nothing from the horrors of Nazi Germany where that nation's leaders sought and received court help to "purify" their country of "defectives."

With courts unrestrained by the actual language of the written law, judges are free to roam wherever their individual beliefs may take them. As our nation moves further away from what Francis Schaeffer calls a "Christian consensus," we will see more and more court decisions at even greater odds with Judeo-Christian values and based instead on pragmatics, hedonism, and materialism.

When human life in and of itself is no longer considered precious simply because we are created by an infinite God; when we value life only in terms of its functional value to society, we can fairly predict that many people's lives are in serious jeopardy.

As a Probate Judge, I have conducted numerous court hearings for mentally ill patients who are being hospitalized involuntarily. I will never forget one day when I was conducting hearings for chronically ill patients at a long-term psychiatric hospital. One patient was too ill to come to the courtroom located at the hospital, so we held court at the patient's bedside in the hospital's geriatric ward.

As I conducted the hearing around the patient's bed, I noticed another woman patient in an adjacent bed. This woman, with a mindless expression on her face, was propped up in her bed for feeding. A hospital staff person, noticeably disliking her duties, tied a large cloth around the patient's neck and attempted to feed the woman by forcing her mouth open and quickly inserting a spoonful of food. The woman repeatedly slobbered much of the food all over the cloth and made a general mess of things.

Watching this pathetic sight, I could not help but ask myself, "What *good* is this woman patient to her society?" Here she was filling an expensive hospital bed costing taxpayers more than $100 per day and producing nothing. It probably wouldn't take much to convince a modern court that "for the good of society" this woman should be put "to sleep." A court-appointed guardian could be obtained to assure the court that, if his client were able to choose, she certainly would agree to end her "meaningless existence."

As resources get scarcer, as medical costs increase and as there are fewer and fewer working people to support the growing elderly population, we can expect that this *will* happen.

But how will our courts be able to disregard the clear words of the Fourteenth Amendment which unequivocally say that no one can be deprived of "life. . .without due process of law?" Rest assured, if the courts can give us abortion on demand and take away the life of a *born* baby in Bloomington, they certainly can find a way to end life for anyone not experiencing a "meaningful life."

TWELVE

Reining in a Runaway Judiciary

BY NOW, THE ALERT READER will be asking the obvious question: how did the Supreme Court get away with it? Since the Court's only authority to declare laws unconstitutional is based on the Constitution itself, how did it manage to strike down anti-abortion laws when the Constitution says nothing about abortion.

The answer to this reasonable question will not be overly pleasing: the Court simply *did* what it did. We citizens through our silence have acquiesed in the Court's decision. The national media has not been silent, however: they have been overwhelmingly supportive of judicial activism in general and abortion on demand in particular.[1]

The scattered criticisms against abortion by individuals and groups are seldom given much positive exposure or emphasis in the media. As a result, no groundswell of public outrage has been generated. And since most of us rely on our media to tell us about any significant problems or injustices that may exist in our country, we've been lulled into silence. Life goes on for the living and the unborn continue to die.

So what can the citizenry do to reverse judicial tyranny? Later I will answer this question more specifically for the Christian citizen. Here I want to examine what all citizens should do to restore the balance of power in our government and regain the essential liberty which our forefathers purchased for us at great personal cost.

In the specific area of abortion, it has been suggested that we pass an amendment to the Constitution to override the Supreme Court's decision legalizing abortion.

I strongly support any method to rid our country of the shameful scourge of abortion, including passage of the Human Life Amendment. But, in some ways, an amendment begs the essential question. To pass a Human Life Amendment would, in effect, tell the Court: "You were right in saying that the Constitution gave the right to abortion on demand, so we had to change the Constitution to eliminate this right." This would also embolden the Court to continue its judicial legislation, knowing that if it gets too far out of line, the people will eventually remedy the situation with another amendment.

Perhaps we could curb the Court's abuses through a different constitutional amendment which would permit Congress to reverse an action of the Supreme Court by a two-thirds vote of both houses. This would only apply when the Supreme Court had declared a federal or state law unconstitutional. Lower court decisions which did the same could be overturned by a simple majority vote of both houses of Congress. In neither case would the President be allowed to veto the action of Congress.

Another idea is to secure an amendment which would allow the discipline or removal from office of Supreme Court Justices and lower court judges for violating the sense of the Constitution or for other misdeeds. The present constitutional standard for the removal of judges is considered too cumbersome; judges can be impeached only for: "Treason, Bribery, or other high Crimes and Misdemeanors."[2]

Another amendment would require elections every six years in which we would vote on whether to retain justices and judges. If a particular justice or judge did not receive a majority vote, he or she would be "banished from the realm" and not allowed to serve as judge again. The amendment could also provide that Congress would have the power, with a two-thirds vote, to recall any of our justices or judges for any reason whatsoever.

I see many advantages and some disadvantages to all of these approaches.

However, there is currently no substantial public momentum favoring the passage of these constitutional amendments. As a result, they are unlikely to be passed at this time.

So we need another way to generate public support to stop our runaway courts. Let's look at the problem from the perspective of the way our government is *supposed* to operate.

We are supposed to have a government "of the people, by the people and for the people." We are said to be a self-governing nation in which the people rule themselves. Our federal government is to have *limited* powers. We have been taught that we will have liberty only so long as we continue to have a "government of laws" rather than a "government of men."

These revered concepts become only so many hollow and trite words describing a bygone era when we consider what the justices of the Supreme Court have been doing. Insulated from direct contact with the citizenry whom they supposedly serve, in office for life like kings of old, the justices have literally been passing laws based on what they *feel* is right, oblivious to the actual language of the document they are supposed to be construing. Is there any question that our forefathers who fought the English in the Revolutionary war would use the word "tyranny" to describe this situation? Certainly, Thomas Jefferson would call it that based on the following quote attributed to him:

> You seem. . .to consider the judges as the ultimate arbiters of all constitutional questions; a very dangerous doctrine indeed, and one which would place us under the despotism of an oligarchy. Our judges are as honest as other men, and

> not more so. They have, with others, the same passions for party, for power, and the privilege of their corps. Their maxim is "*boni judicis est ampliare jurisdictionem*," ["what is good for the judges is splendid for their jurisdiction"] and their power the more dangerous as they are in office for life, and not responsible, as the other functionaries are, to the elective control. The Constitution has erected no such single tribunal, knowing that to whatever hands confided, with the corruptions of time and party, its members would become despots.[3]

The Declaration of Independence is *the* primary philosophical cornerstone for our nation. Few people have read the Declaration in its entirety; even fewer are aware that it describes a view of government which we ignore at the ultimate price of our liberty.

Consider anew the stirring words of this document for which brave men put their all on the line:

> We hold these truths to be self-evident, that all men are created equal, that they are endowed by their Creator with certain unalienable Rights, that among these are Life, Liberty, and the pursuit of Happiness. That to secure these rights, Governments are instituted among Men, *deriving their just powers from the consent of the governed.* That whenever any Form of Government becomes destructive of these ends, it is the Right of the People to alter or to abolish it, and to institute new Government, laying its foundation on such principles and organizing its powers in such form, as to them shall seem most likely to effect their Safety and Happiness. (emphasis added.)

According to our Founding Fathers, all governments in general, and certainly our government in particular, derives its just (as opposed to unjust) powers from the *consent* of the governed.

Our *public servants* (a term we definitely must use more) sitting on the U. S. Supreme Court have absolutely *no* real authority to act apart from what powers we the governed have given to them with our explicit consent. The Constitution itself was the primary means by which we citizens transferred limited power to our government. But who among the readers of this book (who together with the other citizens of this country are the *real* authorities of our land) have ever given their consent to their servants on the Supreme Court to twist the words of the Constitution to the point of saying that women may kill their unborn offspring with total impunity until birth? Not one of you!

At least one justice of the Supreme Court seems to doubt that the *people* of this country are its ultimate authority. In a speech to law students at the University of Kansas in Lawrence, Kansas in April, 1983, Justice Blackmun said that all nine justices of the Supreme Court, "are *prima donnas* in every meaning of that word." He also said of the Court: "It is the end of the line. The buck does stop here. That is the awfulness of the Court's power."[4]

The Court's power is indeed "awful," but Justice Blackmun is wrong to say the "buck" stops with the Court. The "buck" stops ultimately with the *people.* The people don't serve the Supreme Court; the Supreme Court is to serve the people of this country by following the law. This it has *not* done.

As Senator Sam J. Ervin, Jr., defender of our constitutional system, wrote:

> The Founding Fathers did not contemplate that any Supreme Court justice would convert his oath or affirmation to support the Constitution into something worse than solemn mockery. On the contrary, they contemplated that his oath or affirmation. . .would implant indelibly in his mind, heart, and conscience a solemn obligation to be faithful to the Constitution.
>
> A Justice who twists the words of the Constitution awry

> under the guise of interpreting it to substitute his personal notion for a constitutional precept is contemptuous of intellectual integrity. His act in so doing is as inexcusable as that of the witness who commits perjury after taking an oath or making an affirmation to testify truthfully.[5]

But how do we the citizens communicate our displeasure to our public servants on the Supreme Court?

The First Amendment to our Constitution declares:

> Congress shall make no law. . .abridging. . .the right of the people peaceably to assemble, and to petition the Government for a redress of grievances.

We citizens have the right "peaceably to assemble" and to "petition the Government for a redress of grievances."

We have the right and really the duty to tell our public servants on the Supreme Court that we want them to follow the law as written, not as they would like it to be written.

The most effective way to communicate this to the Court is for millions of citizens peaceably to travel to Washington and respectfully yet firmly present our cause to our public servants on the Supreme Court consistent with the First Amendment cited above.

The impelling issue is abortion. We must demand that the Justices follow the law, which will inevitably result in a reversal of *Roe* v *Wade*. To be effective, at least *two million people* must march to Washington. Each of us should carry ten other signatures on a petition insisting that "legal" abortion end. The media will not be able to ignore such a gathering, though some will no doubt dismiss it as a "right wing reactionary backlash to some progressive yet controversial Supreme Court decisions."

As a follow-up to such a "peaceable assembly," someone should challenge Justice Blackmun or Justice Powell to a nationally televised debate on the subject of whether or not the

Constitution really mandates abortion on demand. If no one more knowledgeable volunteers to debate one of the justices, I will volunteer. I would be shocked if a justice would be willing to "face the nation" in this way since the Court is so wrong in its position on abortion. However, I would sincerely relish the opportunity to present the *facts* about the law of abortion to the people of this land. Such a debate challenge, however, will not be effective until the two million of us have peaceably assembled in Washington to rivet the attention of the American people to the issue.

A march on the Supreme Court will generate pressure for change. Momentum will grow. There will soon exist a climate favorable for the passage of constitutional amendments limiting the Court and outlawing abortion. But until this momentum is generated, little if anything will happen to stop abortion in this country.

Let us close this section with a most relevant quote from Abraham Lincoln in a speech in 1859: "The people of these United States are the rightful masters of both congresses and courts, not to overthrow the Constitution, but to overthrow the men who pervert the Constitution."[6]

THIRTEEN

The Christian's Response

THESE LAST FOUR CHAPTERS are written primarily for Christians. I don't mind if those who are not yet total believers in Christ also read this section, but it is expressly aimed at men and women who have already made the conscious decision to take God at his word as expressed in the Bible.

Christianity has gotten a lot of bad press in recent years. Some of it is deserved due to the foolishness of certain Christians, but much criticism of Christians arises more from a hostile social and intellectual environment.

This hostility is reflected in the media. The mere terms used by the media to describe those men and women who take God at his word and live by faith in him have negative connotations. When a news article or TV report calls someone a "fundamentalist believer" or a "born-again evangelical," we are conditioned to think that this is an unsophisticated person whose mind has been programmed by some TV preacher.

The media has made a similar attack on Roman Catholics, especially concerning the fight against abortion. It's as if their opposition to abortion doesn't count because they have made a religious instead of a rational decision to oppose abortion. The implication is that if you are a Roman Catholic or a "fundamentalist," your input to society is of no value. In fact, it would be most appropriate to take away your vote and give it to a "thinking" person if that were possible. Franky Schaeffer does an excellent job of describing this sort of discrimination in his book *A Time for Anger: The Myth of Neutrality.*[1] I recommend reading it.

The reality is very different. A true biblical Christian is ***not*** an ignoramus, but the most creative, imaginative, courageous, charitable, cheerful, and rational person in the world. This may not seem to describe many Christians you know, but it is true.

Why do I say this. Every thinking person at some point in his or her life will consider some basic philosophical questions. Why is the universe so orderly? Where did we come from? Is there life after death? Why is man such an enigma — so amazing in his abilities and love for beauty and relationships, and yet also so cruel and selfish? Who was Jesus Christ who claimed to be God in the flesh and the Savior of mankind?

The one who becomes a true Christian is someone who has courageously and directly faced these and other basic questions. He does not ignore the big issues. Nor does he escape the anxiety these questions produce through the use of alcohol, drugs, fleeting intimacies, entertainment, or any other diversions.

The one who becomes a true Christian has concluded that the Bible's answers to these questions are much more reasonable than the answers provided by any other system. He or she finds that the "God-shaped vacuum" in his or her heart is met by an intimate knowledge of God through his personal emissary to man — Jesus Christ.

The historical person Jesus made some phenomenal claims about himself during his relatively short stay here on planet earth. Read the Gospel of John to see for yourself. There is no way we can regard him as merely a "good man" as many well-intentioned persons do. He is either a liar, a lunatic, or the one he claimed to be — the Son of the living God.

A person becomes a true Christian by entering into a transaction with God whereby the person trades his sin or badness in God's eyes for Jesus' goodness and accepts this exchange personally by faith. The Bible puts it this way:

> For you know the grace of our Lord Jesus Christ, that though he was rich, yet for your sakes he became poor, so that you through his poverty might become rich.
>
> (2 Cor 8:9.)

Why would God be so "foolish" to trade his goodness purchased by Jesus' death on the cross for the garbage of sin in my life? I can glibly say that God did it because he loves the world (John 3:16). But that answer only produces another question: why is he so loving? I'm not sure we will ever fully know the answer to this question. But how fortunate we are that there is a God, and that he is a God of love!

This is the theology of God's love — the theory. But the best thing is that when the Christian theory is applied to someone's actual life, it works! What the Bible says will happen to me *does* happen when I become a Christian.

My life as a true Christian is significantly different from my life when I disregard God and his word. As I trust in God and depend on the many promises in the Bible, I can do things which are humanly impossible for me to do by myself. Without God I would not wish to be the father of eight children nor a juvenile court judge and especially I would not want to be involved in the fight against abortion. But with him, I know I can totally depend upon the Lord Jesus Christ to empower me to do the impossible.

Being a true Christian gives a person the absolute inner assurance of an eternity with God. But the Lord also gives us answers to vexing problems here on earth, family problems, social problems, and others. The Bible is full of our Creator's principles for a proper operation of our lives. However, to the extent we live by our own set of rules oblivious to or in rebellion against his principles, we will be disciplined by the natural and supernatural consequences of our behavior.

For emphasis, let me repeat: it is not following a moral code that makes us true Christians in God's eyes. We become true Christians only as we make the exchange listed above, giving God our sin in exchange for his goodness and righteousness won by Jesus Christ in his sacrificial and historical death on the cross and historical resurrection from the dead. As I make this personal transaction with God by courageous and creative faith, I become a new person. (See 2 Cor. 5:17.) In fact, God in His three personalities, the Father, the Son and the Holy Spirit, comes to dwell within me (see John 14:17,23) and begins to reconstruct my life from the inside out. I soon discover that I want to change my habits that displease him. Also the Bible takes on a new meaning. And when I pray, I know that I am heard. A change has taken place.

To learn more about these basics, read Josh McDowell's books, *More Than a Carpenter* and *Evidence That Demands a Verdict* and C. S. Lewis's books, especially *Mere Christianity.*[2]

As God rules more and more in our lives, we begin to see that he has principles of life not only for individuals, marriages, and families, but also for churches, governments, and nations.

As we carefully study scripture we can develop a biblical view of government and an understanding of the Christian citizen's responsibility with respect to his government.

FOURTEEN

A Biblical View of Government

CHRISTIANS ARE CONFUSED ABOUT the legitimate place of government and the responsibility of Christian citizens in our society. Some Christians honestly believe that all government is under the authority of the devil and that Christians should avoid it altogether. Other Christians believe the opposite —that human government will inevitably usher in heaven on earth. The real truth lies somewhere between these extreme positions.

As Christians, we are compelled to grapple with the responsibilities of citizenship. As in all areas of our lives, we must look to the Bible as the source book of wisdom. The Bible has much to say on the subject.

One author who has been particularly helpful to me in understanding what the Bible has to say about government and Christian citizenship is Samuel Rutherford (1600-1661), author of *Lex Rex, or The Law and the Prince.*[1]

Written in 1643, *Lex Rex* consists of 44 questions and answers about the nature of government and a citizen's rights and responsibilities in regard to it. *Lex Rex* is difficult to read today. Its archaic style and language makes the King James Bible read like a first grader's beginning primer. Yet the book is worth the effort.

Lex Rex profoundly affected the thinking of John Locke. Locke, in turn, influenced the thinking of those who wrote the Declaration of Independence and ignited the American Revolution. As we patiently study *Lex Rex*, we can understand why it heavily influenced our past history and why it has the power to affect our country's future history as well.

Rutherford wrote *Lex Rex* to answer a book written by John Maxwell, an excommunicated Bishop in Scotland. In his book, Maxwell defended the Divine Right of Kings and tried to establish the principle that God demands blind obedience by citizens to their sovereign king's will. Rutherford takes Maxwell's arguments apart piece by piece and buries them under Bible-centered logic.

During the 1600's, Protestant Christians in Scotland were much persecuted by the government. Rutherford's book provided a philosophy whereby the people could resist such persecution. It was a very popular book. But because of its impact, *Lex Rex* was ordered burned. Any person found with a copy was to be considered an enemy of the government. Rutherford himself was deprived of his church and university offices, placed under house arrest, and charged with high treason.

Rutherford died of illness before the government could execute him. A brief biography of Rutherford found in the preface to *Lex Rex* states:

> On his death-bed he was cheered by the consolations of several Christian friends, and on the 20th of March 1661, in the sixty-first year of his age, he breathed his last, in the full assurance and hope of eternal life. His last words were, "Glory, glory, dwelleth in Emmanuel's land."[2]

The following are some of Rutherford's basic principles about government and the Christian citizen:

1. No one is born a governmental leader. Every man is equal in importance in God's eyes. No man is required by God to

obey any other man by nature. All men are born free.

2. However, due to sin, God has ordained human government to preserve man just as God has ordained authority in the family to preserve the family.

3. The *office* of the king or leader comes as an institution of God. However, the *persons* to fill these offices are to be appointed by the people who are governed.

God works through the citizenry to "elect" its leaders. God does not force a leader on an unwilling people. Rutherford provides many illustrations of this principle from the Bible.

For example, Samuel the prophet anointed King Saul to be king (1 Sam 10:1), but Saul did not become king until he was made such by the people (1 Sam 11:15). Similarly, Samuel anointed David king (1 Sam 16:13), but this anointing did not make David king of the land. The people actually made David king in two stages. The first occurred for his reign over Judah alone when he was crowned in Hebron (2 Sam 2:4); the second stage occurred seven and one-half years later for his reign over all of Israel (2 Sam 5:3,5).

Other examples of God allowing the people to select one person instead of another to be their leader can be found throughout the Old Testament.

By contrast, God chose prophets and priests without any help from the people. The people had no say in the selection of Elijah or Jeremiah as prophets. But when it came to their king, God worked through the desires of the people to select the leader.

4. When they choose a leader, the people explicitly delegate some of their innate, God-given authority to rule themselves to their leader. But the people never delegate *all* their authority to the leader. They may properly withold some authority or make the giving of their authority contingent upon the leader complying with certain restrictions or rules. In other words, when people select a leader, they do not give him a blank check to become a tyrant.

Even David, the greatest of Israel's kings, made a "compact" with the people when they crowned him (2 Sam 5:3).

This idea of a compact or covenant resembles our Constitution. The king or leader may be rebuked, challenged, or resisted when he assumes authority ***not*** given to him by the people through their covenant.

5. We obey a king or leader not because the leader is better than we but because God commands obedience to those in authority. We are really obeying God when we obey a leader.

Similarly, a wife does not subject herself to her husband because he is smarter or better than she but because she makes a conscious, voluntary decision to obey God who has commanded obedience to her husband. (Eph. 6:22).

6. The principal duty of the King or leader is to protect the citizens under his care. The leader who intentionally or negligently harms his citizens is not acting in consonance with his calling as a leader.

7. When God mandates obedience to governmental authority in Romans 13, he is not compelling blind obedience to whatever decree the leader may issue. This is a very important issue among Christians. Let us explore it in greater depth. Romans 13:1-5 reads as follows:

> Everyone must submit himself to the governing authorities, for there is no authority except that which God has established. The authorities that exist have been established by God. Consequently, he who rebels against the authority is rebelling against what God has instituted, and those who do so will bring judgment on themselves. For rulers hold no terror for those who do right, but for those who do wrong. Do you want to be free from fear of the one in authority? Then do what is right and he will commend you. For he is God's servant to do you good. But if you do wrong, be afraid, for he does not bear the sword for nothing. He is God's servant, an agent of wrath to bring punishment on the wrongdoer. Therefore, it is necessary to submit to the authorities, not only because of possible punishment but also because of conscience.

Some conclude from Romans 13:1 that God directly ordains human leaders without any input from citizens, making this passage contrary to point #3 above. Romans 13:1 states that "authorities that exist have been established by God."

But this does not preclude God working through the people to select a leader for them. Scripture says a number of times that God did something where it is clear from the context that God worked through the *people* to do it. For example, in Hosea 2:8, God is speaking and says, "I was the one who gave [Israel] the grain, the new wine and oil." Does this mean that God gave this food without any work on the part of the people? Did God just drop these items in their laps? Of course not. Certainly the source is God, but he worked through people to accomplish his will.

Similarly, Romans 13:1 must be interpreted in the context of the rest of scripture which *does* support the concept of God using the "votes" of the people to choose a certain person to be the leader.

We must also interpret Romans 13:2 in the context of the rest of scripture: "Consequently, he who rebels against the authority is rebelling against what God has instituted, and those who do so will bring judgment upon themselves."

This clearly does not mean that we must do *anything* authority commands. Will God's judgment come regardless of what it is the authority has commanded? For example, if the authority orders one man to kill another for no reason, can it be said that to resist this action is to rebel against God? No, rebellion against this order is not true rebellion. The governmental authority has no power to revoke God's law.

We see the difference between righteous and unrighteous authority in Romans 13:3: "For rulers hold no terror for those who do right, but for those who do wrong. Do you want to be free from fear of the one who is in authority? Then do what is right and he will commend you."

This describes righteous authority. When the authority punishes wrongdoers and rewards those who do good, the authority speaks and acts with the very delegated authority of God himself. However, when the authority punishes the innocent and praises the evil, it is blasphemy to say the authority acts for Almighty God. Such leaders deserve God's judgment and are not deserving of passive obedience.

Romans 13:4 explains further: "For he is God's *servant* to do you good. But if you do wrong, be afraid, for he does not bear the sword for nothing. He is God's *servant*, an agent of wrath to bring punishment on the wrongdoer." (emphasis added.)

The ruler is God's *servant.* The Greek word here means the same as "deacon." In other words, the civil authority is to do God's bidding in serving the people. When the civil servant ceases to be under God's law, he ceases to have God's authority to rule. Deuteronomy 17:14-20 relates how God required that a new king make his own copy of God's law and read it daily to learn to revere the Lord and to learn to obey. The result would be that the king would "not consider himself better than his brothers."

Romans 13:5 concludes: "Therefore it is necessary to submit to the authorities, not only because of possible punishment but also because of conscience."

When government serves God by punishing evil, we must obey it or else we sin against God. But if the ruler commands us to sin, we violate our consciences to obey the ruler.

Remember the words of Peter and the other apostles when they were commanded to stop telling others about Jesus: "We must obey God rather than men!" (Acts 5:29)

Obviously, God and civil authority don't always speak in unison.

8. Resistance to civil authorities can be true obedience to God. But the *manner* of resistance must always be consistent with God's principles.

Rutherford develops a priority of resistance. Resistance should begin with *words* or *verbal protest* where appropriate. David attempted this means through his friend Jonathan who tried to appeal to the authority of King Saul, but to no avail

(See 1 Sam 20:12-33). Words are really resistance. Blind obedience does not permit any dialog or discussion or challenges to the leader's orders.

The second step is *fleeing* in self-defense if verbal appeals have been unsuccessful, impossible, or inappropriate. Elijah fled from Jezebel; David fled from Saul; Joseph and Mary fled into Egypt rather than submit to King Herod; Paul was let down in a basket and escaped from Damascus rather than be killed. Fleeing is definitely resistance since the one who runs frustrates the purposes of the civil authorities.

Finally, if verbal appeals fail and fleeing is either unsuccessful or impractical, the next step is the use of physical, forceful *defense* to protect one's self or family or group. David demonstrated this by taking Goliath's sword from the priests and gathering his band of men around him(1 Sam 21:8-9; 22:1-2; 23:13). If his only goal had been to flee, he wouldn't have taken these additional actions.

9. The injunction in I Peter 2:19-25 to submit and suffer patiently under unjust punishment does not mean that self-defense is never appropriate. The passage merely indicates that if we have no choice but to suffer, it is better to suffer patiently than impatiently. This would include the many brave martyrs of the church in times past and currently in parts of the world today. However, we are never to take revenge. The resistance, where possible, must be *only* for self-defense or the defense of other innnocent people who are in danger of imminent, serious bodily injury.

The example that Jesus provides is unique. He voluntarily laid down his life in obedience to God. God nowhere commands that we universally ought to commit self-murder by allowing ourselves to be killed without resistance where resistance in an appropriate form is possible. Such is sin. Let's also recall that Jesus in laying down his life for us was, in reality, taking a sacrificial action for the well-being and salvation of millions of believers. It was no action of a masochist or a suicidal person.

A father who takes steps to kill his children, or the husband who points a loaded gun at his wife, can and properly should be resisted by his children and wife. In doing so, they do not violate Biblical commands of obedience. The father or husband who takes these sinful actions does not represent God in his use of authority; he represents only his own sinful self. And sin must be resisted, especially when it involves hurt to innocent people.

It is no different when a king seeks to kill an innocent subject. The murderous king ceases to be representing God's authority and merely represents himself as a sinful bully who lawfully should be stopped from his crime.

Let's apply these biblical concepts to some real life situations in recent history:

When Hitler and Stalin obliterated millions of innocent citizens in their countries in this century, they were not acting for God. They were merely sinful men with a satanic passion for doing grave injustice.

To resist these monsters with all the force that could be mustered (as the Allies did against Hitler), served God. The Christian should have absolutely *no* pangs of conscience in so doing. Resistance requires courage and it might result in imprisonment or death. But it would be *right* from God's point of view. To do nothing when something can be done is to acquiesce in Satan's plan of killing. To say, "since government which is ordained by God is ordering it, God must be willing it, so I'd better not resist," is to cooperate with evil. This the Christian *cannot* do.

To acquiesce in the evil of abortion because the government declares it legal likewise is to cooperate with evil.

This is particularly true in our country in which ordinary citizens are its ultimate authority.

It meant one thing to be a citizen in Paul's day when citizen participation in the decision-making process of government was neither sought nor welcome. But it means something else to be a citizen in America where we *can* have a profound impact on shaping governmental policies and laws.

It is not good Christian citizenship to justify political ignorance and non-involvement by hiding behind biblical passages that suggest on the surface passive obedience to government. Remember that these verses were written in the context of an empire run by a dictator. Samuel Rutherford's indepth biblical analysis gives a rationale for ultimate citizen control of leaders regardless of the form of government—dictatorship or democratic republic. But even if Rutherford does not totally convince you of his position, certainly it cannot be fairly disputed that an American citizen has not only the opportunity but the ***obligation*** to do what God calls him to do in influencing government. By law, we citizens share the authority in this country with our public servants.[3]

In *The Last Battle*, the final book in the seven-volume *Chronicles of Narnia*, C. S. Lewis provides us with a perfect illustration of governmental authority which should have been resisted, but wasn't.[4]

In Narnia, a great lion called Aslan is the good deity worshipped and obeyed by the good people and animals of the land. In *The Last Battle*, a conniving ape named Shift coerces a gullible donkey named Puzzle to wear a lionskin on his back. The ape's purpose is plain: since lions are rare and the real Aslan is generally invisible, Shift knows he can fool the Narnian creatures into thinking that his donkey in a lionskin is the real Aslan. As the lion's "prophet," Shift can effectively rule the land for his own selfish ends.

The Narnians fall for the ruse. They obey the ape even to the extent of allowing innocent creatures to be mercilessly killed at the ape's command.

The Narnians should have resisted the ape. But they were fearfully intimidated by what they felt was legitimate authority, even when that authority caused death, slavery, and destruction. They had been trained to obey God, but were careless in discriminating between the true God and evil rulers. The real Aslan would have them rebel against Shift and punish him and his lionskinned donkey for their blasphemous behavior.

Would you obey an ungodly despot who orders you not to share your faith with others? I certainly hope you wouldn't. The idea of resistance seems very foreign to us Christians who have had it drummed into our heads from infancy that it is always "good" to obey the authorities. We will not be able to disobey without some ambivalent feelings. But, obviously, to resist would be right. Our feelings are not the final arbiter of what is right and wrong; God's word is. We walk by faith, not by sight or feelings. Let's not lose track, however, that resistance must always be done in the appropriate manner: first verbal protest, then flight if possible, then defense.

In summary, just because a government tells its citizens to do something does not mean the command comes from God. Government in general, and our government in particular (with our Declaration of Independence and the Constitution) is established by the *people* who delegate some of their liberty to their leaders. We the people have never given our government the authority to perform injustice upon our people.

When a leader oversteps the bounds of his delegated authority, when he injures innocent people, when he rewards those who do wrong, he must be restrained and rebuked by the ultimate authorities — the people. A leader has God's blessing only to the extent that he remains a servant of God and his word. As the leader departs from this standard, he becomes a donkey with a lionskin on his back. Such a leader may be intimidating. But he is not powerful unless the people swallow the lie.

Should we be intimidated by men and women in black robes who pretend to speak for God, but in reality speak only for their own minds and desires and create laws that result in the killing of millions of innocent unborn children? God forbid.

FIFTEEN

Steps To Eliminate Abortion

IT'S EASY TO SUGGEST ACTIONS Christians can take to resist abortion in our country. But more important than right actions are right *attitudes* or the deep motivations of our hearts. Attitudes are what we *are*; actions are merely what we do. Actions flow from our attitudes.

As a juvenile court judge, I know that if a wayward young person acquires the proper attitudes, eventually proper actions will follow. But the person who tries to impress others with the right actions without the supporting attitudes will frequently revert back to wrong actions when no one is looking.

My experience overwhelms me with the truth that we parents speak to our children most convincingly by our attitudes. Our actions are somewhat less significant, and our actual words are the least effective means of communication to our children.

Similarly, Jesus said we Christians are the "salt of the earth" (Mt 5:13), which is like the *conscience* of our culture. If this is true, why weren't we Christians more effective in *preventing* abortion from becoming legalized in our country in the first place. I personally believe it is because, in the past, our attitudes relating to abortion and our resulting actions and words were not wholly consistent with God's word.

To eliminate abortion, therefore, we need to check our attitudes to ensure they do conform to God's standards. It is essential that we consider our attitudes in three areas: our attitude toward government, our attitude toward God himself, and our attitude toward children. Let's discuss these one at a time.

Our Attitude Toward Government

We should be grateful to God for government. God uses government as his servant to punish evildoers and reward those who do what is right. With man as sinful as he is, there is a need for the restraining influence of government in our world.

However, when government abdicates its proper God-given role of punishing evil and rewarding good, when it becomes merely a big bully with a gun, doing and encouraging evil, we need not obey it. We must obey God.

We must not eagerly search for opportunities to disobey. Our attitude must be one of respect, loyalty, and gratefulness for the authorities that God has put in our lives. Disobedience must only come after we have prayerfully and with the counsel of others sought "creative alternatives."

When we see a conflict between God's principles and civil authority we can often find a creative alternative that permits us to obey both God and the authority. We saw how Daniel did this when pagan authorities ordered him to eat and drink food that God prohibited. He could have defied the king and probably would have been executed. However, he proposed an alternative that allowed him and his friends to obey God and government at the same time.

Later in Daniel's life, however, he was ordered to pray only to the King. He could see no alternative and had to disobey the rule of man for the sake of God's principles (Dan 6:10)

In fighting abortion, we Christians should be wise like Daniel, yet never so cautious that we lack the courage to be hated, if need be, for the sake of God. One of the best illustrations in scripture of God-honoring attitudes toward government is found in the story of the young nation of Israel living in captivity in Egypt.

In the first chapter of Exodus, we learn that: "The Israelites were fruitful and multiplied greatly and became exceedingly numerous, so that the land was filled with them."

There was a real population explosion of Jews in Egypt. So Pharoah initiated a "birth control" program. The Israelite midwives were instructed to kill all newborn boy babies, but they could allow the girls to live. This law appeared reasonable: the land was already filled with Jewish people; even the Jews should be glad to be able to concentrate on their *quality* of life now. Right? No, wrong!

The midwives defied Pharaoh: "The midwives, however, feared God and did not do what the king of Egypt had told them to do; they let the boys live."

Pharaoh asked them why this was happening, the Israelite midwives *lied*: "Hebrew women are not like Egyptian women; they are vigorous and give birth before the midwives arrive."

To lie like this is *real* resistance against civil authority. But God approved the midwives' resistance: "So God was kind to the midwives, and the people increased and became even more numerous. And because the midwives feared God, he gave them families of their own."

Pharoah's final attempt at population control was to require the drowning of all male children after birth. This rule likewise produced resistance to Pharoah and courageous obedience to God. Were Moses' parents right in breaking the law to keep Moses alive? Without doubt. His parents are listed in the "Hall of the Faithful" in Hebrews 11:23: "By faith Moses' parents hid him for three months after he was born because they saw he was no ordinary child, and they were not afraid of the king's edict."

Isn't it interesting that it's by *faith* that we disobey the government for the sake of our ultimate obedience to God?

Note that the parents saw that Moses was "no ordinary child." There is no such thing as an ordinary child — each child is a unique creation of an infinite God.

If Pharoah had our modern technology of abortion or involuntary birth control, is there any doubt he would have used it? Would the Israelites have been right to resist these efforts in obedience to God? Of course.

Never forget the fact that we obey government not because rulers are better or smarter than we. We all are creatures created in the image of the living God. We submit to government because God commands us to. But when God clearly commands one thing and government unmistakably tells us something else, we can be assured that the ruler is speaking for man, not for God.

Our Attitude Toward God

To eliminate abortion, we need the right attitude toward God himself — the central person of the cosmos.

What does our attitude toward God have to do with fighting abortion? Everything. It's only as we are rightly related to God that we will develop the courage, endurance, and love necessary to keep working until the job gets done.

Most American Christians would be ***shocked*** if someone suggested that their attitude toward God was other than exemplary. But let's be honest. Too often we set our standards by the people around us rather than God's word.

What attitude should we have toward God? That's an easy question. Jesus said the greatest commandment was to: "Love the Lord your God with all your heart and with all our soul and with all your mind" (Mt 22:37).

If asked whether we love God, most of us would respond, "Sure, I love God." But do we love him with ***all*** our heart, ***all*** our soul and ***all*** our mind? Probably not.

Fortunately for us, the Bible gives us some practical ideas on how to love God as we should.

One way in which this is done is to compare our love for God with our love for the things of this world. We are commanded *not* to love the world.

The apostle John says in I John 2:15,17:

> Do not love the world or anything in the world. If anyone loves the world, the love of the Father is not in him. . .The world and its desires pass away, but the man who does the will of God lives forever.

James tells us:

> You adulterous people, don't you know that friendship with the world is hatred toward God? Anyone who chooses to be a friend of the world becomes an enemy of God. (James 4:4).

Similarly, recall Jesus' parable of the sower. Some of the seed is scattered among thorns, which choke out God's work and our fruitfulness. Jesus tells his disciples that the thorns represent those things that draw our hearts and minds away from God: the "worries of this life," "the deceitfulness of wealth," "the desires for other things," and "riches and pleasures." (Mt 13:22; Mark 4:19; Lk 8:14). Note the list includes both things we normally consider good and those we consider bad.

In Matthew 6:19-34, Jesus also shows the connection between our worries about material things and our storing up treasures on earth. He wants us not to serve or love *things* but to serve and love *him*. We are to lay up our *real* treasures in heaven. Jesus made the alternative very clear:

> No one can serve two masters. Either he will hate the one and love the other, or he will be devoted to the one and despise the other. You cannot serve both God and Money. Therefore I tell you, do not worry about your life. . .
>
> (Mt 6:24-25)

As we love and trust God as our provider who meets our needs, we will not worry. Therefore, one test of our love for God is whether worry interferes with our daily lives. If it does, we probably are setting our treasures on earth and our heart is dutifully following this choice (Mt 6:21).

In Colossians 3:1-4, the Apostle Paul tells us what our priorities should be:

> Since, then, you have been raised with Christ, set your ***hearts*** on things above, where Christ is seated at the right hand of God. Set your ***minds*** on things above, not on earthly things. For you died and your life is now hidden with Christ in God. When Christ, who is your life, appears, then you also will appear with him in Glory. (emphasis added).

The point is clear. We are to focus our hearts and minds on our ***real*** home in heaven and on the overseer of that home —the Triune God.

We are to be like the great men and women of faith chronicled in Hebrews 11. They refused to dig their roots deeply into the soil of this decaying world; they realized they were "strangers and pilgrims" on this earth. They sought for their heavenly country (Heb 11:13-16).

But, with all this emphasis on heaven, won't we Christians be ineffective on earth? No. Here is the paradoxical truth: the more we love God and long for our heavenly home, the more we will be persistently and courageously and lovingly free to be creative and powerful change agents here on earth!

I used to think that a person could be so "heavenly-minded that he was no earthly good." I no longer believe this. The person that truly is no earthly good is the "double-minded man" referred to in the book of James (Jas 1:8; 4:8). This is the man who tries to live with one foot in heaven and one foot on earth, who seeks to live for God and seeks to live for himself at the same time. He is the "lukewarm" Christian spoken of in Revelation 3:14-22 who is so nauseating to God. Better to be an all-out sinner; better still to be red-hot in our love for God and his Kingdom. The double-minded man puts on airs of false piety that neither please God nor truly aid those in distress.

Who had a greater impact on our world's history (other than Jesus) than the Apostle Paul? Yet he reminded the Philippians that, "our citizenship is in heaven" (Phil 3:20). He also revealed the greatest desire of his heart:

> I consider everything a loss compared to the surpassing greatness of knowing Christ Jesus my Lord, for whose sake I have lost all things. . .I want to know Christ and the power of his resurrection and the fellowship of sharing in his sufferings. (Phil 3:8,10)

It was *because* Paul had his heart in heaven that he could withstand persecution and pain and deprivation on earth.

To us in America, the world is probably a greater temptation than it was for Paul. We have the resources to attempt to build a heaven on earth. In so trying, we can easily neglect to think about our true home in heaven.

The temptation is particularly intense for Christians who engage in political activity. Some Christians put their focus on eliminating poverty, war, and injustice. Others work to restore a biblical morality in this country so God will bless us with prosperity. These are good goals. But it is wrong to make them *the* goal. Our primary call is not to make the world a nicer or more comfortable place to live in, but to work tirelessly for God out of a heart of love and obedience.

The world may well become more comfortable if we obey God, but God reserves the right to do otherwise (Heb 11:35-38). We should not try to make a heaven on earth; we should set our sights on God's heaven as our real home and work tirelessly to obey him during our relatively short time on earth.

Mother Teresa once told a man who said he wanted to work with lepers, "Brother, your vocation is not to work for lepers. Your vocation is to belong to Jesus."

Let's apply her words to ourselves. Our primary vocation is not to work against abortion. Our vocation is to love and obey God because we belong to Jesus.

We have much to learn from our Christian brothers and sisters behind the Iron Curtain.

A friend of mine recently returned from ministering to some Christians in an Eastern European communist country. He said that most citizens he saw on the streets were noticeably lacking in joy; they have few freedoms and no money to buy "fun" as we define it in America.

The exception, said my friend, are the Christians in that country. They are grateful for life itself. They exude joy, love, and hope. They don't have the money even to try to make a heaven on earth, so they spend time getting to know their Heavenly Father with whom they will spend an eternity. Their attitude makes these Christians extremely courageous to disobey laws which prohibit owning Bibles, conducting in-home prayer meetings, and other necessary Christian activities. These Christians truly have much to teach us in America.

It was obviously this godly sort of attitude that prompted the devout Christian William Wilberforce to enthusiastically work against slavery in England in the late eighteenth century. The slave trade was a well-entrenched, profitable part of the English economy when Wilberforce, a member of Parliament, led the fight to end this cruel, demeaning practice. He encountered bitter opposition and criticism from many fellow countrymen, particularly from the wealthy upper class. The established churches in England accused Wilberforce of being ultra-pious. But when discouraged, Wilberforce was known to re-read a letter written to him by John Wesley when Wesley was eighty-seven. The letter said: "unless God has raised you up for this very thing, you will be worn out by the opposition of men and devils. But if God be for you, who can be against you."[1]

John Quincy Adams also worked tirelessly to eliminate slavery, particularly after he served as President of the United States from 1825 to 1829. After holding the United States' highest office, Adams did not consider it beneath his dignity to carry on his fight as a "lowly" member of the House of Representatives for seventeen years. He was shunned by the elite in Massachusetts and often criticized by the press for his stand against slavery. In the 1830's Adams spoke so often about the blight of slavery that the pro-slavery members of Congress imposed a gag rule on him disallowing action or discussion on his anti-slavery petitions.[2] His personal relationship to God gave Adams the tenacity to continue his fight for what he knew to be right.

Slavery in the early nineteenth century was the sort of issue abortion is today. It was not something an "in" person should get all that upset about. People should have the "freedom of choice" whether to have slaves or not. "Don't impose your moral values against slavery on other people who feel differently." Familiar words about a slightly different subject.

Fortunately Wilberforce, Adams, and Abraham Lincoln persisted for God's sake until slavery was ended. But each man, humanly speaking, paid a price by bearing the ridicule, hatred, and contempt of others.

We all love to receive honor and glory and praise for our work. We like to see our name and hopefully even our picture in the newspaper. I promise you that if you become active in opposing abortion, you will either be ignored or maligned by the press. But if we work for God's approval, he will help us develop thick skin so that we can endure the abuse of men. (See Heb 12:2-3 for the example of Jesus.)

Drawing close to God and setting our hearts on heaven will also soften our hearts so that we will love those whom God loves, including the unborn. James 1:27 says it well: "Religion that God our father accepts as pure and faultless is this: to look after orphans and widows in their distress and to keep oneself from being polluted by the world."

Who could be more an "orphan in distress" than a fragile, despised unborn boy or girl dodging the swipes of the surgeon's knife in a D & C abortion?

Also let us never forget one of Christ's beatitudes as he

describes an aspect of the spirit-filled life of righteousness: "Blessed are the merciful, for they shall obtain mercy." (Mt 5:7)

Working to stop the more than 4000 intentional killings per day of innocent unborn babies in this country is an ultimate act of mercy and love for those whom God himself loves.

Our Attitude Toward Children

Finally, to eliminate abortion, we need the right attitude toward children.

Our society professes to love children, but, with legalized abortion, it should be clear that this love is very conditional and shallow.

More prevalent in our country is a genuine anti-child attitude that ultimately gives rise to abortion on demand. This anti-child attitude does not expressly hate children to the point of wanting to kill them. Rather, it is more subtle. It says:

> Children are an inconvenience to my lifestyle now. Children are an excessive expense and a pain to raise. They prevent me from realizing my potential. For the good of my family and myself, I want my children to be planned. Since I an now pregnant with an unplanned child, I should take steps to end my pregnancy.

By contrast, what does God say about children?

Children are a reward. Children are planned by God. Children enrich our lives (at least spiritually, if not materially). (Pss 127:3; 139:16; 127:4). And children can be used in our lives to help us grow more Christlike (Rm 5:3-5; Jas 1:2-4,12).

American Christians have absorbed more than their share of the worldly attitude that children are inconvenient burdens instead of "blessings." We are prompted to make our lives on earth sufficiently comfortable and easy that we can manage adequately without God's help. We oppose abortion, but many of us tend to agree with pro-abortionists that children are an expensive burden to be minimized if not avoided altogether.

We can see this anti-child attitude behind an official policy statement of the General Assembly of the Presbyterian Church USA:

> In most pregnancies, the question of abortion will never arise, but when it does, the choice of abortion can be an expression of responsibility before God.[3]

We should not be suprised at this policy. It is a natural outgrowth of the anti-child attitude that tragically is very prevalent among Christians.

If the only thing the world hears us "prolife" people saying is, "Yes, children are a first-class pain, but if you make the mistake of getting pregnant, you are stuck. You can't kill them," we will *never* change the abortion policies and practices in our country.

Our conviction must be that each child is a unique creation of an infinitely wise and loving God and that we need and want children in our world. God has a special place in his heart for children. So should we.

Thus our hatred against the scourge of abortion should be exceeded in magnitude by our love for children themselves. These two emotions are not antagonistic. In fact, the more we love children, the more we will wish to eradicate abortion. But merely to desire the elimination of abortion without a genuine, personal and sacrificial love for children is hollow, hypocritical, and unpersuasive.

We should take personal inventory of what our attitudes are, seek God's forgiveness if we have wandered from the mark, and ask for his grace to change. Then it is time to act against abortion.

The Christian who is armed with the knowledge of what abortion is and how abortion became the law in our country, who is filled with the Holy Spirit and has the right attitudes, cannot help but take action to eliminate abortion. I am somewhat reluctant to suggest specific steps to combat abortion because I believe that the best stratgeies and tactics have yet to be discovered. What specifically a person does will depend largely on the special gifts that person has.

Some will write articles, books, letters to editors, letters to congressmen, senators, and Supreme Court justices to protest the law as currently promulgated by the Supreme Court. Others will take to the streets to demonstrate and picket in front of the scenes of the killing — the abortion clinics. We must remind the public that two people go into these places but only one comes out alive.

Some demonstrators will talk to the pregnant women waiting for their abortions and attempt to change their minds. Hundreds of lives are being saved in this way in our country. In Chicago, where this courageous activity got its beginning, more than 150 women in a two-month period decided against abortion while waiting their turns in abortion clinics.[4] Obviously this work can be challenging; the clinics don't like the loss of revenue. Some protestors have been harrassed and others have been arrested for trespass in the process of talking to women in the clinics.

We *must* keep the issue before the apathetic citizenry. The best way to do this is to attract the media to cover anti-abortion news. Thus far, the media has not been inclined to do so; but the press cannot ignore a movement that sparkles with creative ideas and contains multitudes of people willing to act courageously on their convictions.

The established right-to-life movement needs a new infusion of enthusiastic people. Join the movement. Read the literature. Apply pressure. Abortion won't go away easily. Abortion is a diabolical, satanic evil which puts millions of dollars in abortionists' pockets. It will not go away without much pressure and a spiritual confrontation.

People already in the prolife movement should ask whether

they can do more. We will definitely need the two million people who are willing to travel to Washington to petition their Supreme Court "for a redress of grievances."

We need people willing to be considered fanatical by their friends and relatives, people who will insist that the whole story about abortion be repeatedly told until momentum to stop this evil begins to build.

We need people who will have the courage to say that sex outside of marriage *has* devastating consequences. The social work community does us a great disservice by referring to promiscuous young people as being "sexually active," a term devoid of moral connotations, placing such behavior on a par with athletics.

We need less emphasis on contraception and "squeal rules" for young people and more emphasis on proclaiming that God's standards really *are* for our own good as individuals, families, and as a nation. It is loving, not repressive, to preach the Ten Commandments to a fallen world. We violate our Creators' standards to our peril.

We also need to show loving mercy to pregnant girls and women for whom carrying their babies to term will be a significant physical, financial, or emotional burden. Christians should be in the forefront of families and groups providing homes where these women can live. Christians should help develop alternatives to abortion like adoption, foster care, and financial assistance.

We need pro-child/anti-abortion art, music, poetry, and drama. We need to keep peppering our newspapers with letters to editors. We need articles and books and movies. Whatever your skill, we need it!

I do not know what God wants you to do in this area. But God does. If you single-mindedly desire to serve him, he will give you the wisdom you need to know what to do (Jas 1:5-8).

I am personally convinced that if every Christian in our country does what God wants in this area, abortion on demand will soon be abolished.

SIXTEEN

Abortion's End Is Near

IN THE PAST, I have been in despair about the wanton killing of the unborn. More recently, however, as I pray about abortion — individually, with my family and with our church — God has given me the faith to believe that the days of legalized abortion on demand in the United States are numbered.

I continue to grieve about the millions of deaths, but I am also consoled in the conviction that, with God's intervention and through our collective efforts, abortion will indeed end as a "legal" practice in our country.

My encouragement began to blossom as I have seen many Christians (including myself) putting aside wrong attitudes and taking on God's mind about abortion. When other Christians follow, there is no way abortion in this country can continue.

I am further encouraged when, every night, as I listen to my children say their prayers, without any prompting at all, I hear even my three-year old pray, "Help abortion to stop, Jesus." I ***know*** God hears and is going to answer these precious, heartfelt prayers!

These are exciting days in which to live. I am convinced that the annals of heaven will chronicle the lives of many twentieth century Christians who "through faith conquered kingdoms, administered justice, and gained what was promised (Heb

11:33). God is moving in our world and in our land for his great glory. It's exciting to be a part of it!

Let me end this book by quoting from what I feel could well be the Christian's theme psalm in our fight against abortion and our love for children. To my mind, no single chapter of scripture better describes our God-directed struggle than Psalm 94:

O Lord, the God who avenges,
O God who avenges, shine forth.
Rise up, O Judge of the earth,
pay back to the proud what they deserve.
How long will the wicked, O Lord,
how long will the wicked be jubilant?

They pour out arrogant words;
all the evildoers are full of boasting.
They crush your people, O Lord;
they oppress your inheritance.
They slay the widow and the alien;
they murder the fatherless.
They say, "The Lord does not see;
the God of Jacob pays no heed."

Take heed, you senseless ones among the people;
you fools, when will you becme wise?
Does he who implanted the ear not hear?
Does he who formed the eye not see?
Does he who disciplines nations not punish?
Does he who teaches man lack knowledge?
The Lord knows the thoughts of man;
he knows that they are futile.

Blessed is the man you discipline, O Lord,
the man you teach from your law;
you grant him relief from days of trouble,
till a pit is dug for the wicked.

For the Lord will not reject his people;
he will never forsake his inheritance.
Judgment will again be founded on righteousness,
and all the upright in heart will follow it.

Who will rise up for me against the wicked?
Who will take a stand for me against evildoers?
Unless the Lord had given me help,
I would soon have dwelt in the silence of death.
When I said, "My foot is slipping,"
your love, O Lord, supported me.
When anxiety was great within me,
your consolation brought joy to my soul.

Can a corrupt throne be allied with you—
one that brings on misery by its decrees?
They band together against the righteous
and condemn the innocent to death.
But the Lord has become my fortress,
and my God the rock in whom I take refuge.
He will repay them for their sins
and destroy them for their wickedness;
the Lord our God will destroy them. (emphasis supplied.)

To which may we all add our hearty amens!

Judge Hekman's Opinion in the Matter of Jane Doe

STATE OF MICHIGAN
IN THE PROBATE COURT FOR THE COUNTY OF
KENT JUVENILE DIVISION

In The Matter
of
DOE, Jane

Juvenile Court No:28337

OPINION OF THE COURT

I do reserve the right to edit the opinion which I will now be delivering. The edited opinion will take the place of the oral opinion which the Court is delivering.

(The following is the edited opinion of the Court.)

The Court will first address the relatively simple issue of placement. Based on the testimony, the Court finds that the relationship between mother and child has fallen apart, that the mother by her own admission has excessively high expectations for her teen-age daughter which has resulted in a breakdown in their relationship. Mother acknowledges that she needs to make changes in this regard. Mother's lack of parenting skills have been longstanding. This is not the first time that we have seen mother involved with this court; she likewise neglected one of Jane's siblings a few years ago. Approximately one week ago, Jane left her mother to reside in shelter care. It continues to appear that the best interests of Jane would be served if we follow the recommendations of Mrs. Bush that Jane be placed in the neutral setting of a foster home. The Court will so order.

The Court will now address the much more difficult issue of whether or not to grant the requested abortion. The Court finds that there is little or no disagreement by any of the parties with the basic facts. The Court finds that Jane became a temporary ward of the Court on August 18, 1982. Mother appeared with counsel and agreed to the petition alleging that the mother emotionally neglected Jane. The Court accepted the mother's agreement to the petition and adjourned disposition until this date, October 19, 1982. The child, Jane, is 13 years and 5 months at this point. As I have already indicated, mother has been in this court on prior occasions with another child. It's not that the mother intentionally wishes to neglect her children. She simply has her own limitations psychologically, psychiatrically and emotionally which result in a real inability on her part to parent a young teenage daughter.

At the hearing on August 18, 1982, the Court heard from Protective Services worker Barbara Bush who testified that the child had recently run away from Child Haven two different times before being replaced in her mother's home. As of August 18, the child had been in the mother's home for approximately two weeks, and thus far, things were going well. The recommendation was to attempt to work with mother and child at home with Bethany Christian Services providing on-going counseling. At the August 18 hearing, Jane also appeared but was quite uncommunicative — similar to her demeanor today. At that first hearing, there was absolutely no hint whatsoever of Jane being pregnant. Since the placement was somewhat dubious in light of past problems, I decided to adjourn disposition until today.

According to the Protective Services report available to the Court at this time, which is Exhibit 1 received into evidence, Mrs. Doe called Barbara Bush on September 13, 1982, stating that she felt her daughter was five month pregnant at that time. Mother enrolled her daughter in Park School, a school for pregnant teenagers. As far as specifics, according to Exhibit 1, it would appear that Jane was 15 weeks pregnant as of September 10, 1982, which would put her very close to 20 weeks pregnant at this moment in time. According to the testimony and according to the psychological report of Dr. Thomas Duthler, Exhibits 2 and 3, the father of the child that Jane carries is a 13 year old unnamed friend. Mother, in her testimony, indicated that it's possible that the father is a cousin of Jane. Again, there is no conclusive proof on this point: Jane refuses to acknowledge to the caseworker who her child's father is.

On September 16, 1982, Park School called Protective Services and indicated that the child wanted her pregnancy "terminated." As a result, Planned Parenthood was consulted at that time.

On September 29, 1982, the child told Barbara Bush that she wanted an abortion. Mother expressed to Mrs. Bush that she was totally opposed to her daughter having an abortion. Mrs. Bush checked into different abortion clinics and learned, among other things, that no abortion could be performed on this girl absent parental authorization or court order.

Also, on September 29, Mrs. Bush contacted this Court and talked to my case aide, Mrs. Deborah Kammer, seeking direction. Mrs. Kammer and I discussed the issue at that time. Since this was a case of first impression for me, I noted a statute MCLA 722.124a(3); MSA 25.358(24a) (3) which I initially felt was controlling in this matter. This provision states very specifically that, ***the minor child's parent or legal*** *guardian shall consent to nonemergency, elective surgery for a child in foster care.*" (emphasis supplied). And only if parental rights are terminated, may the Court consent to that nonemergency, elective surgery. From the facts in this instant case, an abortion definitely would be deemed "nonemergency, elective surgery." While this was my initial reaction to what the law is in this area, a more thorough examination of the applicable case law since that date convinces me to take a different point of view.

Nonetheless, based on my preliminary assessment of the law, I instructed Barbara Bush on September 29 that we as a court did not have the authority to order an abortion and that the decision was between the girl, her physician and her parents. On October 13, 1982, Attorney Lou Hoos informally saw me between court hearings here at the courthouse and indicated "a tough case" was coming my way. He explained briefly that his client, Jane, wanted an abortion to which her mother was objecting. Therefore, he was filing a motion to obtain court authorization for the abortion. I asked him for any input on the legal issues, but he was equally unfamiliar with any legal precedent in this area of the law. Mr. Hoos indicated that he had learned just a week before that his client was in fact pregnant.

A dispositional hearing was set in this matter for today, October 19, at 9:30 a.m. and intended to take one half hour. However the one half hour was, of course, scheduled before we knew that we were going to have to decide the weighty issue of abortion in addition to the relatively simpler issue of placement.

On October 18, 1982, this court received a Petition to Obtain Court's Permission for Abortion filed by Mr. Hoos on behalf of his client. There were no legal citations accompanying the petition whatsoever.

Based on all the testimony that the Court has received, including witnesses and exhibits, the Court finds that Jane, at the age of 13 years and 5 months, is slightly subaverage in intelligence as compared to the norm for her chronological age. She has by no means satisfied this court that she is mature and well informed enough to make intelligently the abortion decision on her own. There is no testimony to the contrary. Futher, it would appear from all the testimony that her reason for wanting the abortion is for personal reasons that she has not shared with caseworkers. Mother testified that Jane told her she thought the father of the unborn child was a cousin and Jane was concerned the child to be born would in some way be handicapped. This is the first this court has heard this suggestion from anyone. Perhaps it is the first anyone in the court other than the mother has heard this statement. Nonetheless, it appears that Jane is requesting the abortion not for medical or physical necessity, but for other personal reasons known to her alone.

All the evidence received by the Court on the issue, from Paul Cartwright of Protective Services and Exhibits 1, 2 and 3 unanimously support a finding that it is in Jane's best interest to carry the child to term and not have the abortion. Jane did not offer any testimony to the contrary either by herself or through other witnesses.

As indicated before, this is the first case of this type that has come to the Kent County Probate Court as best I can determine through conversations with other Kent Probate Judges. The law for a case such as this is very unclear. In general, we know that since the Probate Court is of limited jurisdiction, we must look to statutes for direction and authority.

The section of law mentioned earlier, MCLA 722.124a(3); MSA 25.358(24a) (3), makes it clear that whether a child wishes to have her ears pierced or whether she wishes a therapeutic, elective, nonemergency abortion, she needs parental consent despite the fact that she may be a ward of the Juvenile Court and placed in foster care. I find that this particular statute modifies Juvenile Code Section 712A.18(h) which allows the Court to "provide a child with medical, dental, surgical or other health care in a local hospital or elsewhere. . .as the court deems necessary." While a plain reading of this latter provision would suggest a Juvenile Court Judge could order *any* medical care including elective, non-emergency surgery, the more specific provision of MSA 25.358(24a) (3) takes precedence. Obviously, our legislature intends that parents retaining parental rights continue to have the authority to make cosmetic and other discretionary medical decisions for their children. Apparently, most other states have similar laws requiring parental consent for surgery on their minor children.

However, the United States Supreme Court has carved out a significant exception to the general rule of needing parental consent in the specific area of abortion. Parents may constitutionally veto any surgical procedure for their child except that child's abortion. The cases which support this general principle are *Planned Parenthood of Central Missouri* v *Danforth* 428 US 52, 96 S Ct 2831, 49 L Ed 2d 788 (1976) and *Bellotti* v *Baird* 443 US 622, 99 S Ct 3035, 61 L Ed 2d 797 (1979). I'm not going to try to defend the logic of the Supreme Court in carving out the abortion exception to the general rule that parents must consent to cosmetic or elective surgery for their children. I, frankly, would have a difficult time doing so.

Nonetheless, it is clear from the holdings of *Danforth* and *Bellotti* that the U. S. Supreme Court would find MSA 25.358(24a) (3) unconstitutional to the extent that parents can effectively veto their minor daughter's desire for abortion. The justices in *Danforth* voted 5 to 4 in striking down a Missouri statute that required parental consent as a prerequisite for a minor's abortion.

In *Bellotti*, 8 of 9 justices agreed to declare a Massachusetts statute unconstitutional which required parental input and notice to parents when a child sought an abortion. Certainly, if that court found it unconstitutional simply to notify parents of the child's desire for an abortion, it would certainly find unconstitutional a requirement like is contained in our statute for parental consent as the condition precedent to any abortion.

Hence, it appears to this Court that MSA 25.358(24a) (3) is unconstitutional in that it allows parents effectively to veto the decision of a minor child to obtain an abortion.

That being the finding of this Court, however, does not end our inquiry into the law. Having struck down a statute as unconstitutional does not tell us what procedure should be substituted in its place where a 13 year old is seeking an abortion and her mother strenuously opposes the same. Unfortunately, the Supreme Court is not much help in this regard.

In *Danforth*, 5 of the 9 justices held that, ". . .we agree that the State may not impose a blanket provision. . .requiring the consent of a parent or person *in loco parentis* as a condition for abortion of an unmarried minor during the first 12 weeks of her pregnancy. . .the State does not have the constitutional authority to give a third party and absolute, and possibly arbitrary, veto over the decision of the physician and his patient to terminate the patient's pregnancy regardless of the reasons for withholding the consent."

This holding is problematic in two regards: 1. It was specifically limited to abortions sought during the first trimester of pregnancy (which we definitely do not have in the instant case here); and, 2. More essentially, the Supreme Court held that no third party, no person acting *in loco parentis*, could legally have an absolute veto over a girl and her physician's decision to abort.

Is not the juvenile court a third party acting *in loco parentis*, or which is alternatively stated as the *parens patriae* for children —especially for those children in foster care?

If I read *Danforth* correctly, the Supreme Court is saying that all third parties, parents and others — including courts —must keep out of this very private decision to be made by a pregnant girl and her physician.

The Supreme Court in *Danforth*, however, somewhat relaxes its position when it closes this section of their opinion by stating, "We emphasize that our holding does not suggest that every minor, regardless of age or maturity may give effective consent for termination of her pregnancy."

In trying to mesh together this latter statement with the prior holding that a third party can't be an absolute veto to a minor's abortion, we must ask what procedure is intended by the Supreme Court for immature minors? While it doesn't specifically say, we can safely speculate that someone apparently has the authority to effectively veto the abortion of an immature minor under certain, but totally unknown conditions.

Let us now examine *Bellotti* v *Baird*. While *Bellotti* has all the external earmarks of giving a trial court some criteria to use in the place of our unconstitutional statute, in reality it does not. Only 4 of 9 justices agreed on what we will call the lead opinion in *Bellotti* which established a two-pronged inquiry for a court: 1. A minor seeking an abortion without parental consent must convince a court that she is mature and well-informed enough to make intelligently the abortion decision on her own. If she succeeds, the court must authorize her to act without parental consultation or consent. 2. If the girl fails to satisfy the court that she is competent to make this decision independently, she must be permitted to show that abortion would nonetheless be in her best interest. If the court is persuaded that it is in her best interest to have the abortion, the Court must authorize same. If not, the court may decline to sanction the operation.

While there are some problems with the above scheme, it is theoretically workable.

However, let's remember that it was a *minority* of the Supreme Court that decided the case in this fashion. Another four justices who joined in declaring the Massachusetts statute unconstitutional specifically refused to agree with the procedures outlined in the lead opinion. In fact, the 4 justice second opinion was extremely critical of allowing a judge to have the veto power since his decision "must necessarily reflect personal and societal values and mores whose enforcement upon the minor. . .is fundamentally at odds with privacy interests underlying the constitutional protection afforded to her decision." The ninth justice (Justice White) dissented altogether as he has on all the abortion decisions.

A decision by the U. S. Supreme Court that does not garner a majority vote of that court has no precedental value nor is it binding to other courts. *People* v *Anderson* 389 Mich 155.

Almost one year ago to the day, on October 20, 1981, U. S. District Court Judge Benjamin Gibson of the Western District of Michigan handed down the case of *Pelletier* v *Halstead.* In his opinion, Judge Gibson ordered Judge Halstead to apply the criteria of the four justice minority lead opinion in *Bellotti.* Even if Judge Gibson's ruling had been based on a more solid foundation than the dubious precedent of *Bellotti*, the decision of a single federal district court judge concerning another probate judge on different facts is not binding to this probate judge on these facts. *Washington* v *Chrysler* 63 Mich App 156; *Knight* v *Tecumseh* 63 Mich App 215, 219.

Hence, we are without any clear law to follow.

In light of this confusion, I believe legally I am free to respond in one of two ways: 1. I can do nothing because my authority to act is in doubt; or, 2. I can use some creativity and attempt to fashion a standard to apply in keeping with the principles of law that we do have. I personally think that in a case where time is of the essence, it's wrong to do nothing. In some sense, a bad (should I say an inartful) decision is better than none at all. It at least gets the case moving in some direction so it can be reviewed by other courts if need be. For this reason, I will do my best to choose a procedure which is as consistent with the law as possible.

At least five justices in *Danforth* and four in *Bellotti* would acknowledge some means of veto power over an immature minor pregnant girl based on her best interests. I have already found that we are dealing with an immature minor in our instant case.

With respect to a mature minor pregnant girl, probably a

fair reading of both decisions is that she should, in the Supreme Court's opinion, have access to an abortion without any veto power held by any third party.

Since dividing the issue between mature and immature minors comes closest to the procedures suggested in the lead opinion in *Bellotti*, for lack of any better guidance, this court is going to consider this four justice holding as the law to use at this time. However, I will be quick to point out that this is certainly a case of first impression and purely a stab in the dark by one solitary trial judge who feels that a decision needs to be made promptly.

Bellotti's lead opinion of four justices directs a court to determine whether the pregnant girl is mature and informed enough to make the abortion decision apart from her parent. If so, the court is to authorize her to act without parental consultation or consent. There is no disagreement in any of the testimony that Jane is other than immature, a fact the Court has already found to be true. However, where the child is not mature enough to make the abortion decision herself, the trial court must look to the pregnant girl's best interests which, *Bellotti* indicates, means *her* best interests *alone* with a total disregard of all parental objects "and other considerations which are not based *exclusively* on what would serve the minor's best interest." (emphasis supplied.)

Undoubtedly, this latter phrase means the court can give absolutely no regard for the unborn child in its decision. With this, I have a problem.

For close to eight years, I have been a juvenile court judge. I am trained in this position to show compassion for and enthusiastically give weight to the rights and needs of those who are too weak, infirmed, or helpless to assert their own rights.

When a little newborn baby has been brutally beaten by his mother's boyfriend, I seek to protect that child from further harm. I instinctively come to the aid of mentally impaired citizens; without trying, I desire healing for the five year old sexual abuse victim and take whatever steps I can to obtain this for her. Simply because a party is too weak or nonverbal to stand up for himself or herself really doesn't matter to me: they are, nonetheless, important. In every case in juvenile court my goal is to obtain for each child that which is spoken of in the preamble to the Juvenile Code: "such care, guidance and control, preferably in his own home, as will be conducive to the child's welfare and the best interest of the state."

A case often cited in termination cases is *In re LaFlure* 48 Mich App 377 (1973) which makes it clear that children are entitled to a stable and decent environment in which to mature and that their rights must be considered along with the rights of the parents.

When we come to the law relating to abortion, however it seems that all logic and reasonableness is thrown out the window. I'm asked by the law to totally disregard the poor, defenseless unborn child that grows and moves within his or her mother's womb.

In considering whether or not to place this unborn child on death row to await certain execution, I may look only to whether such action will further the best interests of the pregnant girl who carries the child. I am given no specific criteria as to what "best interests" mean. In fact, the four justice minor opinion in *Bellotti* criticizes the four justice lead opinion for this very reason. "Best interest" could simply boil down to whether the girl would be happier to get this "thing" out of her as soon as possible so she can go back to whatever she wants to do. If I understand the law correctly, therefore, I will need to perform an amazing feat of mental and moral gymnastics which is so totally contrary and foreign to the way we approach all other cases here in juvenile court.

Because of my tension with the law that disallows a judge to have regard for the unborn, I have considered disqualifying myself pursuant to GCR 912. However having examined this court rule, I find I do not fit within any of the criteria for disqualification as I read them. I am not in any way prejudiced for against any party or attorney nor do I fall within any of the other criteria of GCR912. In addition, it is abhorrent to me to conclude that I am somehow handicapped as not being objective or otherwise being, in some way, a substandard type of juvenile court judge simply because I consider life more important than a person's expediency; that I inherently desire to help the underdog, the weak, the helpless; that I consider it not asking too much of a girl to be pregnant for a few weeks more for the sake of keeping another creature alive hopefully for many years. Perhaps, for abortion cases, we need to call on judges who are indifferent to life and have no scruples about arbitrarily ordering the execution of innocent victims when they conclude the pregnant girl's existence would, in some tangible or intangible way, be thereby enhanced. I personally don't know any juvenile court judges in Michigan that could meet this latter requirement.

For all the above reasons, I choose not to spontaneously disqualify myself.

Obviously, inherent in my statements thus far, is my assessment that the unborn child is a person, or at least a living creature whose rights must be considered separately from the mother's.

I am aware that the U. S. Supreme Court has held that until the unborn child reaches the magical point in time called "viability" (which occurs at roughly the 27th week of gestation), the child is legally a nonperson and should therefore be totally disregarded.

But simply because someone is a nonperson does not mean he has no rights. Dogs are nonpersons, but you can be constitutionally prosecuted and punished in Michigan if you are cruel to a dog. This is true even if you are exercising your first amendment rights of freedom of speech by branding a slogan on the side of your dog.

Certainly the pregnant woman is entitled to her constitutional rights. But may she in exercising these rights cause irrepairable injuries — specifically death — to another living creature who is at that time alive and well and innocent of wrong? The Supreme Court in *Roe* v *Wade* 410 US 113, 93 S Ct 705, 35L Ed 2d 147 (1973) was very clever to call the fetus "potential life" which suggests it is an inanimate object not truly yet alive. But who can reasonably contest the fact that the fetus, although perhaps in the eyes of the law not fully a person, is nonetheless fully *alive* as opposed to being in the category of dead? If the fetus were truly inanimate or dead, there would be no raging national debate on the abortion question whatsoever.

While the mother may have the right by the U. S. Supreme Court to get rid of the child she is carrying, does she have a separate right to kill the child who depends on her for life? Simply because abortion and death of the child most often occur at closely related times does not mean that they are one and the same event. The death of the child is only proof positive of how truly defenseless, needy and dependent upon outside care this young life was.

Eventually, the mother will have what she desires — an end to her pregnancy. Is it asking too much of her to carry the child a few more months for the separate rights of that life within?

Before I apply the facts of this case to the law developed earlier in this opinion, I wish to state emphatically that I consider the putting to death of an unborn child far more significant than asking a young woman who is 5 months pregnant to be inconvenienced for a few months more.

Nonetheless, I do find that literally all the evidence in this specific case supports the position that it would serve the best interests of Jane, separate and apart from her mother and separate and apart from her unborn child, for her to carry her child to term and not to have the abortion. However, I want to be "up front" and totally honest with all the parties in this case that if the evidence for the pregnant girl went the other way, I still would not be able to order an abortion in light of the life of the unborn child unless, of course, the abortion was necessary to save the life of the pregnant girl.

If, by so stating my position, I threaten to violate the law of the land as laid down by the U. S. Supreme Court (which, as I mentioned earlier, is less than clear) I choose to do so. I do not say this lightly. I consider my oath of office as a solemn trust. In eight years on the bench, I have not violated that solemn trust and I have no intentions of doing so in the future apart from cases like this that literally involve life and death. Where I am ordered to put to death innocent subjects for the expediency of others, I do refuse and will refuse to so act.

Simply because the U. S. Supreme Court decides that a principle of law is legally right does not make that principle right in the ultimate or absolute sense. Is there nothing above the Supreme Court? Certainly, one might answer, the Constitution is above the Supreme Court. But, as one justice himself candidly said, "The Constitution is what the Supreme Court says it is." To amplify this point, I defy anyone to find the word "abortion" in the entire Constitution. All attorneys well know from the decisions that there is a lot of judicial hand waving and legal gymnastics used to create out of thin air the right of privacy and the related right to an abortion. There are many other decisions of the Supreme Court which I find illogical, but I still follow them religiously due to my oath of office. However, when a decision threatens the life of an innocent being, I must apply a different standard.

Forty years ago in Hitler's Germany it was totally legal to torture, maim, cruelly experiment with and otherwise kill people of Jewish descent.

After the war, these same governmental officials were tried and many were executed according to principles of a higher law.

To quote from one attorney at the Nuremburg trials: "A soldier is always faced with the alternative of obeying or disobeying an order. If he knows the order is criminal, it is surely a hollow excuse to say it must be obeyed for the sake of obedience alone."

There is no question in my mind that if I am ordered to

initiate procedures to kill innocent life for the expediency of otheres, that that is a "criminal order" which I cannot obey.

For the reasons contained in this opinion, the petition for the abortion is respectfully denied.

RANDALL J. HEKMAN
Judge of Probate

Grand Rapids, Michigan
October 25, 1982

Grand Rapids Press Editorial

Sunday, November 7, 1982

Judge Put Self Above the Law

Kent County Probate Judge Randall Hekman is guilty of failure to step aside from a case on which he was biased and probably of blatant pandering to his political constituents.

The dispute revolves around abortion and a pregnant 13-year-old ward of the court. The girl's decision last week to carry the child to term doesn't absolve Mr. Hekman for his injudicious behavior.

After first explaining that his personal beliefs would prevent him from even considering an abortion for the girl, Judge Hekman declined to disqualify himself and rejected the petition of the girl's attorney-guardian.

Surely Judge Hekman knew his ruling, deliberately tainted with bias, would be quickly tossed out and another hearing would be conducted. He also knew he could count on the anti-abortion forces to ignore the legal implications of such cavalier treatment and to champion his courage.

The issue is not about abortion, although many will try to make it such. The issue is the judge's calculated determination that he is not always bound by law or courtroom procedure, or even by the principle that justice must be blind.

And those who would attack Judge Robert Benson, as being pro-abortion in ordering a new hearing, have missed the legal boat completely. Judge Benson's order was a model of judicial restraint in an explosive case.

He agreed with Judge Hekman's analysis of related court cases ("I bow to his expertise in that area"), but added: "If a judge starts out with the premise he cannot under any circumstance grant a petition, he does not exercise judicial discretion. We judges are not really free under our oaths to follow what the law should be. We must follow the way the law is."

In almost any other kind of case, judicial bias of this gravity would be regarded by legal peers and laymen alike as totally unacceptable. But Judge Hekman knew that he was not taking much of a risk.

The circumstances are a reprise of his behavior in a bitterly fought 1974 political campaign. Then, as a relatively inexperienced lawyer, he chose to seek the bench by milking community emotions and fear on juvenile crime. Television advertisements played up the idea that a kid in Juvenile Court could get away with anything short of murder and candidate Hekman hammered away on the "high crime rate among juveniles in Kent County and the permissive attitude of the Juvenile Court."

At his January 1974 swearing-in, he said he was "elected not because I am such a great legal mind but because (my campaign issue) met favorably with the way people in the community think" — delicate language for what some at the time called demagoguery.

He seems not to have lost the touch. In the current case, the judge possessed responsible options that would not have stained his judicial credibility, nor would they have bent his principles on abortion. He could have stated his feelings on the issue — even more strongly if he preferred — and then excused himself, sparing a circuit judge the job of pointing out an obvious judicial indiscretion. Or he could have approached the case with an open mind, eventually spelling out in necessary detail where the Supreme Court had erred on abortion, thus opening up the case to a normal appeals process.

He did neither, flaunting instead a personal bias that could not be ignored by either the public or the girl's attorney.

His motives can only be guessed at, but the consequences, whether anticipated by him or not, are quite clear. He gained substantial publicity on a highly politicized issue and one which could do him no harm among his constituency. And by not excusing himself immediately, he caused delay and increased the risk for the girl in the event she wanted an abortion and was allowed to have one.

Further, in what other cases will Judge Hekman publicly take sides without excusing himself as being partial? Are all judges to be allowed this privilege?

After nearly eight years on the probate bench one would assume that Judge Hekman's grandstanding and quaint notions on his right to prejudge cases had been smoothed over with legal maturity and wisdom. Apparently, they have not.

APPENDIX C

Judge Hekman's Response

Friday, November 19, 1982

Abortion and Justice

The Press editorial of Nov. 7, regarding a 13-year-old pregnant girl whose case came before my court, failed to address some essential issues. Hence, I wish to respond.

The Press' main point was summarized in its headline, "Judge Put Self Above the Law."

The idea of judges putting themselves above the law should be repugnant to all citizens. Who can disagree with the premise that judges are to follow the clear teaching of the law in cases that come before them?

But are there ever instances in which, for the sake of justice, judges should disobey the law? Or do we want our judges always to behave like mindless bureaucrats who dutifully process cases oblivious to the demands of ultimate justice?

What if the law requires a judge to order the execution of a person known to be totally innocent? What if a judge is required by law to order Jewish people to concentration camps or gas chambers because the law says that Jews are non-persons? What if a judge, sitting on a case involving a runaway slave, disagrees with the Supreme Court's 1856 decision in which black slaves were ruled to be nothing more than chattels? Are these not all instances in which judges should take a stand against unjust laws for the sake of doing that which is ultimately right?

Can the judges in these cases escape moral culpability either by obeying the law and saying they were "just following orders" or by disqualifying themselves so that other judges without their scruples can issue the unjust decrees?

Certainly the "just following orders" defense did not work to excuse Nazi war criminals — nor should it have worked.

How about disqualification? If a judge steps aside from a case knowing full well that another judge will be found who is appropriately "unbiased" and who thus will enforce the unjust law, the first judge does not absolve himself from his moral dilemma.

The judge who is required by law to order the execution of an innocent man and who deliberately gives the case to another judge remains a knowing and willing part of the ultimate injustice. However, if the case is taken out of the judge's grasp through the appeal process he cannot morally be faulted; he has done what he could do.

Do these principles apply in a case where a judge is asked to order the killing of an unborn child because the 13-year-old mother, who is five months pregnant, feels this is what she wants? I believe, without question, it does. Let me explain why.

Ten years ago a judge in Michigan would be guilty of a felony crime if he encouraged, much less ordered, that a pregnant girl obtain an abortion. Then, in 1973, the U.S. Supreme Court ruled that all state laws making abortion a crime were unconstitutional. In one day, that which had been a reprehensible crime became a sacred right protected by the Constitution itself.

But not only has the Supreme Court made what was formerly illegal and unthinkable a constitutionally revered and protected right, it has given to trial judges such as myself the responsibility not merely to protect this right for women but actually to order the killing of the unborn.

The Supreme Court never had to order that an abortion take place, only that women could choose an abortion if they so desired. But we juvenile court judges, whose statutory responsibility is the protection of children from abuse, must perform the "hatchet job" of assigning unborn children to a cruel and merciless death when their mothers are immature and cannot legally make the decision for themselves.

What is equally absurd is that in considering whether to order the demise of an unborn baby, judges are required to engage in the mental fiction that the baby is a non-entity.

In the above discussion, I have used the words "unborn baby" and "killing" to describe abortion. Obviously, the whole argument against abortion would fade into nothingness if, in fact, unborn children were only lifeless collections of tissue. However, the more medical science discovers about the development of human beings in the womb the more it describes a jumping, sucking, thriving young boy or girl who, of all the living creatures in the world, most closely resembles a human baby.

In fact, in the very first cell that everyone reading these words once was is contained all the specific information about our ultimate height, color of hair, eyes, our tendency to become diabetic, etc.

The Supreme Court was able to disregard the rights of unborn children by calling the fetus "potential human life" and by saying that this "potential life" is really only a part of the mother's body until approximately the 7th month of pregnancy.

But who can rationally deny that what the Supreme Court has called only "potentially" alive is truly and totally alive as opposed to being in the opposite category of dead? And, medically, there is no question but that this child — even from the first cell being formed — is a foreign body to the mother which must eventually leave her or kill her.

Perhaps abortionists can hide from the truth through the use of euphemisms. But courts cannot do other than face the facts — especially when they are asked to order a deliberate killing of a fellow human being (albeit a rather small person). Since when do we discriminate against people on the basis of their size or attained intelligence or verbal ability or ability to care for themselves?

Since when is the taking of human life merely at the whim of another other than a classical case of injustice?

Is not the case where a judge is asked to order the killing of an unborn child almost identical to our earlier example where a jduge is asked to order the execution of a totally innocent man? I say it is. When faced with this issue, a judge should courageously do what is ultimately right and just by resisting the action which is requested. Transferring the case to another judge will only make the first judge an "aider and abetter" of the ultimate injustice.

While my own decision actually rested on the above principles, there is a plausible legal argument why what I did was not only the ultimately just decision but it was legally correct as well.

Space limitations do not permit me to fully develop my argument. However, the basic question is whether a Supreme Court decision that runs so contrary to the letter and spirit of the Constitution and contrary to the fundamental absolutes upon which our system of laws is based is, nonetheless, a decision that must legally be honored by all lower courts.

There is some legal precedent to support answering this question in the negative. That is to say, an arbitrary decision of a higher court that originates solely in the subjective feelings of those on that court but is contrary to fundamental laws carries with it no force of law whatsoever. This argument had particular force in an age when courts acknowledged the reality of external absolutes; however, in our relativistic society, such is more likely to fall on deaf ears.

Regardless, when a judge is faced with the option of doing that which is ultimately just versus that which is merely legal, he ought to choose the just and be willing to suffer, if need be, the consequences of doing so.

RANDALL J. HEKMAN
Judge of Probate

Notes

Chapter 1
My World Turned Upside Down

1. Michigan Compiled Laws, Annotated 722.124a(3); MSA 25.358(24a)(3).
2. The preamble to the Michigan Juvenile Code reads: "This chapter shall be liberally construed to the end that each child coming within the jurisdiction of the court shall receive such care, guidance and control, preferably in his own home, as will be conducive to the child's welfare and the best interest of the state and that when such child is removed from the control of his parents the court shall secure for him care as nearly as possible equivalent to the care which should have been given to him by them." MCLA 712A.1
3. Psalm 139:13

Chapter 2
My Decision

1. *Roe* v *Wade*, 410 US 113, 93 S Ct 705, 35 L Ed 2d 147 (1973)
2. Michigan Code of Judicial Conduct, Canon 3A. (6)
3. These details about Jane's decision are from a Kent County Department of Social Services' investigation, summarized in an inter office memorandum by Paul Cartwright, Supervisor, Children's Protective Services, November 24, 1982.

Chapter 3
The Judge on Trial

1. In October, 1981, Judge Donald Halstead of Kalamazoo County, Michigan was presented with a petition by the attorney for a pregnant 11 year old asking for Court authority to grant an abortion. The differences in his case were that the girl herself opposed the abortion and she had become pregnant through an incestuous relationship with a person significantly older than she. In my case, the 13 year old *wanted* the abortion and her pregnancy occurred as a result of a relationship with a male peer of hers.

2. I Thessalonians 5:18; Ephesians 5:20; and Colossians 3:15-17.
3. Michigan General Court Rule(GCR) 932.
4. GCR 932.25
5. *San Francisco Examiner*, January 27, 1983; Christian Legal Society *Quarterly*, Vol IV, November 1, 1982; *National Right to Life News*, March 10, 1983; *Christianity Today*, March 4, 1983.
6. *Maher* v *Roe*, 432 US 464, 53 L Ed 2d 484 (1977)
7. *Harris* v *McRae*, 448 US 297, 65 L Ed 2d 784 (1980)

Chapter 4
Life Is in God's Hands

1. According to the autopsy of the boy, his initial Apgars were 8 and 9, but two hours after birth he was floppy and lethargic with fixed pupils and a poor respiratory rate. All the "parts" were there in place. The examiner noted "there is no cleft palate or other defect of eyes, ears, nose and throat. Digits appear to be normal. The external genitalia are normal male." The autopsy continues to describe in intricate detail how well-formed are all the parts of the child's body including the bones, the pancreas, the brain, etc. The only area of concern was the main pulmonary artery leading from the heart to the lungs which was significantly dilated showing evidence of congestion. In effect, the child died of the lack of oxygen in his system.

Chapter 5
The Facts and Morality of Abortion

1. Victor G. Rosenblum, "Abortion, Personhood and the Fourteenth Amendment," Chicago: Americans United for Life, Inc., Studies in Law and Medicine, No. 11, p. 5
2. Ibid. p. 7
3. Ibid. p. 7, quoting from J. Mohr, *Abortion in America, The Origins and Evolution of National Policy* (1978)
4. Ibid. pp. 6-7
5. Draft Report on S. 158 by Dr. Sean O'Reilly, dated July 2, 1981, pp. 29-30
6. The *Grand Rapids Press* reported June 16, 1983 about two different babies born in different cities each born four and one-half months premature. The one child, weighing 16.8 ounces at birth, was going home weighing five and one-half pounds. The treating doctor commented, "Once she got past that first week of life, it was a snap." He added that the child should "grow up to be a healthy child." The other baby was born weighing 18 ounces and was being taken off the critical list at the time of the article. According to the article, *The Guiness Book of World Records* lists Marion Chapman as the smallest baby to have survived. She weighed 10 ounces when she was born June 5, 1938, in South Shields, England.
7. Bernard Nathanson and Adell Nathanson, *The Abortion Papers: Inside the*

Abortion Mentality, Madison, Wisconsin: Idea Inc., 1983
8. John T. Noonan, "The Experience of Pain by the Unborn," *New Perspectives on Human Abortion*, Frederick Md.: Aletheia Books, University Publications of America, 1981, p. 205
9. Ibid. p. 212
10. Rick Edmonds and Liz Jeffries, "Abortion" printed originally in the *Philadelphia Inquirer* August 1, 1981. Quoted in Franky Schaeffer, *A Time for Anger: The Myth of Neutrality*, Westchester, IL: Crossway Books, 1982, p. 181
11. Ibid. p. 156
12. Ibid. p. 161
13. Stanislaw Z. Zembrych, "Fertility Problems Following an Aborted First Pregnancy," *New Perspectives on Human Abortion*, p. 128
14. Ibid. p. 131
15. Ibid.
16. Myre Sim, "Abortion and Psychiatry," *New Perspectives on Human Abortion*, p. 151
17. Ibid. pp. 156-157
18. Ibid. p. 158
19. "Post Abortion Sequelae," a report dated February 1, 1981, by Pregnancy Aftermath Helpline, Inc., 4742 N. Sheffield Ave., Milwaukee, Wisconsin 53211
20. "Out in the Open to Fight Abortion," *Grand Rapids Press*, October 20, 1983, p. 2B
21. Ibid.
22. "Abortion" op. cit., *A Time for Anger*, pp. 169-170
23. Ibid. p. 170
24. *Webster's New World Dictionary*
25. Christopher Tietze, *Induced Abortions, A World Review, 1983*, New York: The Population Council, Inc., 1983, p. 33 shows the numbers of abortions in the U. S. as reported to the Alan Guttmacher Institute. These numbers are considered more reliable than the slightly lower values published by the Center for Disease Control (CDC), since the CDC relies on data from the state health departments which, particularly in the earlier years of "legalized" abortion, were unreliable. The numbers of abortions in the U. S. for 1973 through 1980 are listed as follows:

Year	*Numbers of Abortions*	*Abortions per 100 Pregnancies*
1973	744,600	19.3
1974	898,600	22.0
1975	1,034,200	24.9
1976	1,179,300	26.5
1977	1,316,700	28.6
1978	1,409,600	29.2
1979	1,497,700	29.6
1980	1,553,900	30.0

I have assumed that there are 1.5 million abortions for each year during 1981 and 1982.

26. John Powell, *Abortion: The Silent Holocaust*, Allen Texas: Argus Communications, 1981.
27. Assuming 1.5 million abortions per year, which is probably too low an estimate by now. *Statistical Abstract of the U.S.*, U.S. Department of Commerce, Bureau of the Census, states on page 70 that in 1980 there were 428 abortions per 1000 live births, meaning 428/1428 30% per combination. Tietze, *Induced Abortion*, op. cit., lists 30 abortions per 100 pregnancies in the U. S. in 1980 on page 33.
28. *Statistical Abstract of the U. S.*, op. cit., p. 70, shows the District of Columbia with 1569 abortions per 1000 live births in 1980.

Chapter 6
What the Bible Says About Abortion

1. Keil and Delitzsch, *Biblical Commentary on the Old Testament*, Grand Rapids: William B. Eerdmans, Vol 2, pp. 134-135

Chapter 7
The Arguments for Abortion

1. *Dred Scott* v *Sandford*, 60 US (19 How.) 393 (1857)
2. The Thirteenth (1865) and the Fourteenth (1868) Amendments to the U. S. Constitution.
3. National Committee for Adoption, "Adoption Facts Summary," October 26, 1983, p. 4
4. "The National Study on Child Neglect and Abuse Reporting," The American Humane Assoc., 1981; "1977 Analysis of Child Abuse and Neglect Research," U. S. Dept of HEW, 1978.
5. John Lippis, "The Challenge to Be Pro Life," Santa Barbara Pro Life Education Inc., 1978, p. 14.
6. B. Systa, et. al., "An Objective Model for Estimating Criminal Abortions and its Implications for Public Policy," *New Perspectives on Human Abortion*, op. cit.
7. From an unpublished talk by Professor Basile Joseph Uddo at the Michigan Right to Life Conference, Calvin College, Grand Rapids, Michigan, Sep. 25, 1982.
8. Ibid.
9. Raoul Tunley, "Incest: Facing the Ultimate Taboo," *Readers Digest*, January, 1981.
10. Ibid.
11. "Out in the Open to Fight Abortion," *Grand Rapids Press*, op. cit.
12. *Cosmopolitan World Atlas*, Chicago: Rand McNally and Co., 1961 p. 132
13. Pat Gilliland, ed. *Our Magnificent Earth*, Chicago: Rand McNally and Co., 1979, p. 168
14. Brian P. Price, *Rand McNally Pictorial World Atlas*, Chicago: Rand McNally and Co., 1980

15. Rousas J. Rushdoony, *The Myth of Overpopulation*, Nutley, N. J.: Craig Press, 1969, pp. 1-2
16. "The Population Bomb Threat: A Look at the Facts," in *The Zero People*, Jeff Hensley, ed. Ann Arbor: Servant Publications, 1983, p. 35
17. "U. S. Population: Where We Are; Where We're Going," *Population Bulletin*, Vol. 37, No. 2, June 1982, p. 7
18. *Population Bulletin*, June, 1982, op. cit. pp. 7-8
19. "Grim Future Seen for 'Baby-boomers' born in 1945-1965," *Grand Rapids Press*, October 3, 1983. Also, *Population Bulletin*, June 1982, op. cit. p. 32.
20. *Population Bulletin*, June 1982,op. cit. p.32
21. "Our Population Predicament: A New Look," *Population Bulletin*, Vol. 34, No. 5, Dec, 1979, p. 19
22. *Population Bulletin*, June 1982, op. cit. pp. 33, 45
23. Ibid.
24. *Population Bulletin*, Dec 1979, op. cit. p. 18

Chapter 8
The Power of Judicial Review

1. 1 Cranch 137, 2 L Ed 60 (1803)
2. The Judiciary Act of 1789, 1 Stat. 73
3. A pamphlet obtainable from members of Congress consisting of 20 pages describing the Supreme Court's history and functions. No publication date or publisher is indicated, but presumably is by the Government Printing Office, p. 4
4. *The Federalist Papers, A Contemporary Selection*, abridged and edited by Lester DeKoster, Grand Rapids: William B. Eerdmans Publishing Co., 1976, p. 101
5. Ibid. p. 102
6. Ibid. pp. 100-101
7. *The Antifederalist Papers*, edited by Morton Borden, East Lansing: Michigan State University Press, 1965, pp. 222-223
8. Ibid. pp. 222-240.
9. Ibid. p. 240
10. U.S. Constitution, Article III, Sec 1
11. Justice Thomas M. Cooley, *Constitutional Limitations*, Boston: Little, Brown and Company, 8th edition, 1972
10. Ibid. p. 123
11. Ibid. p. 124
12. Ibid. p. 127
13. Ibid. p. 128
14. Ibid. p. 130
15. Ibid. p. 133; p. 68, footnote 3
16. Ibid. pp. 141-142
17. Ibid. p. 332
18. Ibid. pp. 335-337
19. Ibid. p. 338

20. Ibid. p. 340
21. Ibid. pp. 341ff. There are currently many legal minds who argue that modern life is far too complex and the Constitution too antiquated to require judges in the 1980s to be bound by the actual language of the Constitution. They feel our Supreme Court should be a "continuing constitutional convention," amending the original as society's needs require. They argue that we need some moral and legal absolutes to "fill in the gaps" between Constitutional provisions and to provide a foundation upon which our legal system can be built.

    It is totally true that every society needs absolutes to avoid ultimate anarchy. Laws do reflect a sense of what is ultimately right and wrong. The Supreme Court, therefore, could be viewed as serving a necessary function in promulgating absolutes for our society and our nation's conscience.

    The only problem with this is that the Supreme Court has been issuing its arbitrary absolutes from the basis of sociological factors irrespective of the foundation our system of laws was historically built upon. Any historian of our legal system is aware that the absolute undergirding of our system of laws came from the common law of England and the philosophy underlying our Declaration of Independence. As we consider these two sources, we must conclude that underlying them in turn is the Judeo-Christian tradition. For the Supreme Court to choose other foundations is to switch essential philosophical horses midstream without the consent of the ultimate authorities in the country—the people.
22. Ibid. p. 345
23. Ibid. pp. 345-346
24. *McCray* v *United States*, 195 US 27, 24 S Ct 769, 49 L Ed 78. Cited on page 347 of Cooley, op. cit.
25. Cooley, op. cit. pp. 349ff
26. Ibid. p. 353
27. Ibid. p. 352, quoting *Russ* v *Com.*, 210 Pa St. 544, 60 Atl 169.
28. Ibid. pp. 371-372
29. Ibid. p. 374

Chapter 9
The Growth of Judicial Legislation

1. *Lochner* v *New York*, 198 US45, 25 S Ct 539, 49 L Ed 937 (1905)
2. See Jules B. Gerard, "A Proposal to Amend Article III: Putting a Check on Antidemocratic Courts," *A Blueprint for Judicial Reform*, edited by Patrick B. McGuigan et. al., Washington, D. C: Free Congress Research and Education Foundation, Inc. 1981, p. 233
3. *Erie Railway Company* v *Tompkins*, 304 US 64, 58 S Ct 817, 82 L Ed 1188 (1938)
4. *Cooper* v *Aaron*, 358 US 1, 78 S Ct 1401, 3 L Ed 2d 5 (1958)
5. Arthur Selwyn Miller, *The Supreme Court, Myth and Reality*, Westport,

Connecticut: Greenwood Press, 1978, p. 295
6. *Miranda* v *Arizona*, 384 US 436, 86 S Ct 1602, 16 L Ed 2d 694 (1966)
7. *Griswold* v *Connecticut*, 381 US 479, 85 S Ct 1678, 14 L Ed 2d 510 (1965)
8. Dixon, "The 'New' Substantive Due Process and the Democratic Ethic: A Prolegomenon," 1976 B.Y.U.L. Rev 43, 84
9. *Roe* v *Wade*, 410 US 113, 93 S Ct 705, 35 L Ed 2d 147 (1973). I will quote this decision frequently on the following pages.
10. See John W. Whitehead, *The Second American Revolution*, Elgin IL: David C. Cook Publishing Co., 1982; Victor G. Rosenblum, "Abortion, Personhood and the Fourteenth Amendment," Chicago: Americans United for Life, Inc., Studies in Law and Medicine, No. 11; John D. Gorby, "The 'Right' to an Abortion, the Scope of Fourteenth Amendment 'Personhood' and the Supreme Court's Birth Requirement," Chicago: Americans United for Life, Inc., Studies in Law and Medicine, No. 5.
11. A companion case of *Roe* was *Doe* v *Bolton*, 410 US 179, 93 S Ct 739, 35 L Ed 2d 201 (1973). *Doe* specifically ruled that "health" included more than physical health. "... [The] medical judgment [for abortion] may be exercised in the light of all factors— physical, emotional, psychological, familial, and the woman's age—relevant to the well being of the patient. All these factors may relate to health." *Doe*, supra, at 192.

Chapter 10
An Evaluation of Roe v *Wade*

1. *Roe*, supra, at 153
2. Raoul Berger, *Government by Judiciary*, Cambridge, Mass: Harvard University Press, 1977
3. Ibid. p. 213
4. *The Papers of Alexander Hamilton* 35 (H. C. Syrett and J. E. Cooke, eds., 1962) quoted in Berger, ibid. p. 194
5. The only exception to this statement was a superficial effort by Blackmun to decide whether an unborn child is to be considered a "person" pursuant to the Fourteenth Amendment. Blackmun, in effect, put the burden on the State of Texas for persuading the court an unborn child is a person. However, Blackmun also made Texas carry the burden that "liberty" did *not* include a woman's right to abortion. Should not the burdens of proof on both issues rightly be placed on "Jane Roe?"
6. In his rewriting of history, Blackmun in *Roe* tried to conclude that "it now appear[s] doubtful that abortion was ever firmly established as a common-law crime even with respect to the destruction of a quick fetus." *Roe,* supra, at 136. John D. Gorby convincingly establishes, however, that abortion of a quickened fetus was clearly illegal at common law, citing Lord Coke, Sir William Blackstone as well as modern scholars of the common law. According to Gorby, Blackmun's rewrite of history was aided in no small part by abortion proponent Cyril Means who is

freely quoted by Blackmun in his opinion in *Roe.* (See Gorby, op. cit., pp. 13-15)
7. *The Supreme Court, Myth and Reality,* Miller, op. cit., p. 286.
8. *Human Life Review,* Spring, 1983.
9. John P. East, "The Case for Withdrawal of Jurisdiction," *A Blueprint for Judicial Reform,* op. cit., pp. 29, 34.
10. Testimony of Senator Eagleton before the Senate Judiciary Subcommittee on the Constitution.
11. White's dissent is found in *Doe v Bolton,* supra, (White, J. dissenting)
12. *Roe,* supra, at 174-177
13. Testimony of Judge Bork on the Helms Human Life Bill before a U.S. Senate Subcommittee.
14. Archibald Cox, *The Roe of the Supreme Court in American Government,* New York: Oxford, Va. Press, 1976
15. John Hart Ely, "The Wages of Crying Wolf: A Comment on *Roe* v *Wade,*" 82 Yale L.J. 920, 932, 935-936.
16. Bob Woodward and Scott Armstrong, *The Brethren: Inside the Supreme Court,* New York: Simon and Schuster, 1979, p. 233
17. *The Supreme Court, Myth and Reality,* op. cit., pp. 364-365
18. Terry Eastland, "10 Years After the Abortion Decision," *The Wall Street Journal,* January 17, 1983.

Chapter 11
The Legacy of Roe v *Wade*

1. *Akron* v *Akron Center for Reproductive Health,* 76 L Ed 2d 687, 696-697 (1983)
2. "The Life and Death of Infant Doe," *National Right to Life News,* May 10, 1982, p. 1
3. MCLA 712A.2(b)(1)
4. "Gesell Strikes Down 'Baby Doe' Regulation," *National Right to Life News,* April 28, 1983.

Chapter 12
Reining in a Runaway Judiciary

1. For a clear description of the bias and power of the media elite, see Franky Schaeffer, *A Time for Anger: The Myth of neutrality,* Westchester, IL: Crossway Books, 1982. In particular, on page 27 of his book Schaeffer describes a study showing that 90% of the leading journalists in our country feel a woman should have the right to decide for herself whether to have an abortion.
2. U.S. Constitution, Article II, Sec. 4. the argument to the contrary is that Article III, Sec. 1 of the Constitution says that "The Judges, both of the supreme and inferior Courts, shall hold their offices *during good behavior.*" (emphasis added). It is unclear, however, whether they can be removed merely for "bad behavior" when Article II, Sec. 4 seems to

provide the only method of actual removal of "all civil officers." The question is further complicated by the reality that the Supreme Court would ultimately decide this legal issue.

One must fairly ask, however, whether it is not treasonable for a judge to deliberately and repeatedly violate his oath of office whereby he has pledged to "support *this* Constitution" by actually the ignoring the Constitution as written and construing one that is unwritten.

3. Letter of Thomas Jefferson to William C. Jarvis, September 28, 1820, cited in *A Blueprint for Judicial Reform,* op. cit., p. 353
4. "Blackmun Calls Fellow Justices Prima Donnas," The *Grand Rapids Press,* April 7, 1983, p. 5A
5. Sam J. Ervin, Jr., "Judicial Verbicide: An Affront to the Constitution," *A Blueprint for Judicial Reform,* op. cit., p. 3, 14.
6. *The Life and Writings of Abraham Lincoln*, edited by Philip Van Doren Stern, New York: Random House, 1940, p. 788.

Chapter 13
The Christian's Response

1. Franky Schaeffer, *A Time for Anger: The Myth of Neutrality,* Westchester IL: Crossway Books, 1982
2. Josh McDowell, *More Than a Carpenter,* Wheaton, IL: Tyndale House Publishers, 1977; *Evidence That Demands a Verdict,* San Bernardino, CA: Campus Crusade for Christ, Inc. 1972; C.S. Lewis, *Mere Christianity,* New York: Macmillan Publishing Co., Inc., 1952.

Chapter 14
A Biblical View of Government

1. Samuel Rutherford, *Lex, Rex, or The Law and the Prince,* Edinburgh: Robert Ogle and Oliver & Boyd, 1843.
2. *Lex Rex,* op. cit., p. xix
3. For an excellent discussion of our right and responsibilities as Christian citizens in America, see William Stanmeyer, *Clear and Present Danger,* Ann Arbor: Servant Publications, pp. 52-59.
4. C.S. Lewis, *The Last Battle,* New York: Macmillan Publishing Company, Inc. 1956.

Chapter 15
Steps To Eliminate Abortion

1. John Pollock, *Wilberforce,* New York: St. Martin's Press, 1977, p. 105.
2. Foundation for Christian Self Government *Newsletter,* May/June 1983, Westlake Village, California, p. 5.
3. *Moody Monthly,* September, 1983, p. 8.
4. Pro Life Brotherhood *Newsletter,* September, 1983, 350 S. Orchard Dr. Park Forest, IL 60466, p. 1

grounds [illegible] [illegible] the [illegible] by the [illegible] that the Supreme Court [illegible]
[illegible]

[illegible]

[illegible] *Law and* [illegible]
[illegible], April 7, [illegible]

[illegible] Vol. [illegible], p. [illegible]

[illegible] New York: Random House, 1970, p. [illegible]

Chapter 13
The Christian Response

[illegible] Books, 1983.

[illegible] Wheaton, Ill.: Tyndale House Publishers, 1977. [illegible]

[illegible], Inc., 1978. [illegible]
New York: [illegible] Publishing [illegible]

Chapter 14
[illegible]

1. Samuel Rutherford, [illegible] *Lex Rex, or the Law and the Prince* [illegible]
[illegible]
2. [illegible]
3. [illegible]
[illegible] Ann Arbor: [illegible], p. [illegible].
4. [illegible] New York: Macmillan Publishing Company, Inc., 1980.

Chapter 15
[illegible]

1. [illegible] New York: [illegible] Press, 1977, p. 105.
2. [illegible] June 1983,
[illegible]
3. [illegible]
4. [illegible]
[illegible]